D0443799

Christmas
Miracles

Christmas Miracles

Cecil Murphey *and* Marley Gibson

Foreword by *Don Piper*
Author of *90 Minutes in Heaven*

St. Martin's Press ✿ New York

CHRISTMAS MIRACLES. Copyright © 2009 by Cecil Murphey and Marley Gibson. Foreword copyright © 2009 by Don Piper. All rights reserved. Printed in the United States of America. For information, address St. Martin's Press, 175 Fifth Avenue, New York, N.Y. 10010.

www.stmartins.com

Design by Susan Walsh

LIBRARY OF CONGRESS CATALOGING-IN-PUBLICATION DATA

Murphey, Cecil B.
Christmas miracles / Cecil Murphey and Marley Gibson ;
foreword by Don Piper.—1st ed.
p. cm.
ISBN 978-0-312-58983-7
1. Miracles.   2. Christmas—Miscellanea.   I. Gibson, Marley.   II. Title.
BT97.3.M87 2009
242'.335—dc22

2009016919

First Edition: October 2009

10 9 8 7 6 5 4 3 2 1

A Note to the Reader

Unless otherwise noted, all biblical quotations are from the New Living Translation. These are true stories of Christmas miracles. We've edited them to provide a consistent writing style.

Contents

Acknowledgments

We're both thankful for our agent, Deidre Knight, and for our editor, Rose Hilliard. Both of them enthusiastically encouraged us in this project.

Foreword

I love miracles. They're around us all the time if we can only see them. To see them, however, we must be willing to perceive what's not always obvious.

I define miracles in one of three ways: A miracle is (1) an effect or extraordinary event in the physical world that surpasses known human or natural powers and is ascribed to a supernatural cause; (2) an event that some consider a work of God; or (3) a wonder or marvel that defies explanation.

Miracles come about in many ways. Occasionally we witness a direct intervention by God and the disruption of natural laws as the definition points out. The Bible is filled with miracles and you'll read of a few such events in this book.

Most often, miracles seem to be the matter of perfect timing. Someone has a need, prays, and the answer arrives at exactly the moment it's needed.

Sometimes the miracle is a change of attitude. Maybe it's the help of a kind stranger—or was it an angel? Miracles come in all forms and are a gift from God to let us know that we're not alone in this world. These true stories teach us to reach out and ask for God's help.

Cecil "Cec" Murphey and Marley Gibson have gathered together a collection of miracles. These heartwarming stories occur around the Christmas season. After all, Christmas was when God gave us the greatest miracle of all—his son.

Of course, to accept miracles is a subjective decision. Some might not think that getting money unexpectedly is a miracle, but when it puts a holiday meal on the table or provides toys for your children, it means everything to that family. This book is full of such miracles that will touch your soul, make you cry, and tug at your heartstrings.

I have a story about a Christmas miracle that happened to me.

✳   ✳   ✳

Our Boy Scout Troop 200 scheduled our annual Christmas party. We looked forward to each year's party because we played silly games, ate a lot of food, and even better, we exchanged gifts.

Two weeks before the party, each boy drew the name of another troop member for whom he was to bring a gift. The scoutmasters said we couldn't spend more than five dollars.

We weren't supposed to know who drew our names, but being kids, it wasn't long until each of us knew.

The night of Troop 200's Christmas party arrived and we had a fun time, but the highlight would be the exchange of gifts. It finally came. Under our tree was a stack of gloriously wrapped guy gifts. One by one the scoutmaster picked up a gift, called a name, and we watched the boy tear open his package. We oohed and aahed each time.

When George opened my present to him I watched his face. He beamed in appreciation. I rocked back and forth, feeling good.

What could Randy have gotten for me? He came from a well-to-do family and I was sure he'd give me a really nice gift.

As the gift giving continued, I counted the gifts and the boys. I wasn't positive, but it looked as if we were going to be one or two gifts short. A sagging feeling came over me: *I might not get a gift.* I banished that thought from my mind.

Finally two of us waited. Only one gift lay under the tree. The scoutmaster picked it up.

He called the other boy's name.

There was no gift for me under the tree. It hurt to be sitting there, the only scout without a present. It was also embarrassing. I didn't look around but I was sure all the boys stared at me.

I knew (and so did most of the others) that Randy had drawn my name. Money wasn't a problem. He hadn't forgotten, I thought. He just didn't care.

He can take a gift, but he can't give one. I wanted to cry, but I was too big and too proud to let tears fall in front of the other boys. Like any twelve-year-old boy I smiled and turned to admire the gifts the other boys had. I don't know how effective it was, but I tried.

Just then, Bobby, the assistant scoutmaster, laid his right hand on my shoulders. "Here is your Christmas present." I looked up into his caring eyes. "We saved it for last." He held out his clenched left hand.

Bobby took my hand and placed his on top of mine and

deposited a shiny Walking Liberty silver dollar, bona fide U. S. mint issue, in my palm.

I held it up, smiling. It seemed as if every boy in the room rushed over to admire my silver dollar. And it was beautiful.

As the others told me what a great gift I had received, I remembered something. I had seen that silver dollar before. Bobby kept it in his wallet as a keepsake from his late father.

"I can't take this," I said and held it out for him to take. "Your daddy gave this to you. It's okay, really, I'm sure Randy just forgot to buy me something. It doesn't matter."

It mattered, of course. Bobby understood that, and he wouldn't take it back.

To some, this story doesn't sound like a miracle, but it was to me. I was a hurting kid, who had been overlooked. Bobby's gift was much more than a silver dollar. It was God's loving hand reaching out to me through a sensitive, caring leader.

✳ ✳ ✳

The existence of miracles in our lives is an assurance that we're not alone and that our Heavenly Father looks out for us in our hours of need and even in what might seem to be a trivial situation. It's up to us to open our eyes and recognize the miracles that happen in our lives and be grateful for them. Always.

—DON PIPER

Christmas
Miracles

1. My First Christmas

Cecil Murphey

I SANG WITH THE SMALL GROUP THAT GATHERED AROUND the piano. Shirley, whom I later married, played carols and sang alto. My best friend, John Burbank, had a beautiful tenor voice. Others harmonized so their voices blended nicely. I knew enough about music to realize it sounded better if I moved away and listened.

I walked over to the window and stared into the dark evening. The snow had started to fall shortly after lunch on that Thursday—four days before Christmas. By now, at least two inches had accumulated. The streetlight made the heavy flakes glow as they hit the ground.

Just then, Shirley began to play "O Come, All Ye Faithful." Of all the carols, that was and continues to be my favorite. Momentarily I closed my eyes and listened to them sing. When they finished the third stanza, I asked, "Would you sing it again? Just for me?"

Shirley touched the keys and they sang.

That was one of the most perfect moments in my life. Each Christmas I reflect on that scene. Many years have passed so my memory may not be accurate on every detail. It doesn't matter: That was my first Christmas—the first time I grasped the meaning and the purpose of that holy day.

I was a month away from my twenty-second birthday. I had grown up with a limited exposure to the church during my first eleven years. That's when I decided that church was "for old ladies and dumb kids." I had walked out of a Sunday school class, out of the building, and as far from Christianity as I could. For a decade I never walked inside a church building.

At age twenty-one, my world crashed over an aborted love affair. In my pain, I thought about God, and went to a church service. I'm not even sure why. On my way out, I picked up a free New Testament. I didn't return to that church, but I did read the New Testament.

After months of almost-daily reading, I decided I believed what I read. "If I believe, I need to do something about this," I said to myself. That's when I seriously attended church. I met Shirley and we fell in love. Six weeks before Christmas I was baptized in her church.

As the group reached the crescendo with "Christ the Lord," I smiled. I understood those words. It's not that they had been unintelligible; it was that I had been unable to personalize the Christmas message.

I knew the story—what child didn't? But until that night, the meaning of Christmas had been lost on me. The season had been one of giving and receiving gifts, of constant music in stores, and greetings everywhere of "Merry Christmas." People decorated their houses and sometimes their yards. The theaters released their cheery and sometimes sappy Christmas films.

At home my mother always made mince pie—her favorite, I suppose. Friends gave me gifts and I bought presents for them. In general, people seemed a little nicer and maybe a few degrees happier.

On that Thursday night before Christmas, I *understood*. Christmas is a night of promise—a promise to the entire world. God presented his greatest miracle to the world. In God's quiet way he was saying, "This is to show you my love. I've given you my son. One day he will grow up and willingly die for you. That's how much I love you—enough to give you the most important thing in the universe—a part of myself."

Tears surfaced and I turned away from the group. I suppose I was too embarrassed to let them see my tears. But those were what I called happy tears.

This is my first Christmas. Now I know what it means.

In the years since, I've celebrated Jesus' birth in many places and under varying circumstances. Many of them were special moments for me. But none of them have ever touched me quite as deeply as that first one.

Perhaps that's the reason: It was the first. It was an awakening. From someone who had no interest in spiritual things, God performed a special miracle in my life. That baby was a living love letter to me.

2. Miracle in the Storm

Elizabeth M. Harbuck with Marley Gibson

CHRISTMAS 1967 MIGHT HAVE BEEN A DELIGHTFUL BUT OR-
dinary time except for one thing. Mother and Daddy drove from
Alabama to Massachusetts to spend the Christmas holiday with
us. They traveled in their new four-door Thunderbird, which
was the prettiest car they had ever owned. Before they made the
long trip north, Daddy had it serviced at the local garage.

We had a wonderful time together and did all the seasonal
things. We attended Christmas Eve service at church, wrapped
and later unwrapped presents, talked, joked, baked, and argued
about whether this year's dressing in the turkey was as good as
last year's.

The beautiful white Christmas was perfect for New England. Then the day came for my parents to leave. The snow had
piled high on the ground and the weather reports predicted
more. I was a little worried and asked them to stay.

Daddy wasn't concerned. "I've driven in heavy snow many
times," he reminded us. He also pointed out that they would
drive on the then-new interstate highways. "Besides, I have a
new car and it's in top condition. I don't expect any problems
getting home."

They considered stopping at a motel until the storm blew over, but decided to drive through to Alabama. Somewhere in Connecticut, a blinding snowstorm caught them. Daddy had about a five-foot visibility. He slowed the car to a crawl. They hadn't seen any other vehicles for a long time and no snowplows had come through.

Just then, his right-rear tire blew. The car jolted and thudded as the rim of the wheel took the weight. He pulled the car to the side of the road. The visibility hadn't improved and snow pelted the car. He was weak and feverish. Neither he nor Mother had any idea where they were except somewhere in Connecticut. This happened long before the day of cell phones.

Daddy had a choice: He could wait until someone came along to help—and neither of them had any idea when that would happen—or he could get out in the blizzard and change it himself.

"Sit tight," he told Mother. "I'll change it as quickly as I can."

"Let me help—"

"One of us out in the storm is enough. No sense in your getting sick. Stay inside, pray, and keep warm."

Mother was upset over the flat tire. She also felt concerned about his safety. They had heard terrible stories of people being robbed on the highway. After Daddy got out of the car, she folded her hands together, closed her eyes, and prayed, "Dear God, please help us."

No sooner had Daddy opened the trunk to take out the jack than two young men appeared.

Surprised, Daddy looked up. He had no idea where they came from and didn't see another car. His immediate reaction was, *Oh, they're going to rob us. Maybe kill us.*

"Hello there!" one of them called in a cheery voice.

"Sir, we'll be glad to change the tire for you."

"Thank you, but—"

"Please get back in the car, sir," the second man said. "It's freezing out here. We'll change the tire."

Afraid to argue with them, Daddy nodded and turned back. He got inside the car.

"You haven't changed the tire already?" Mother said.

He shook his head and took her hand. She couldn't see what was going on, so Daddy explained about the two men.

"Do you think it's safe?" she asked.

"I don't know," he said. "But they don't seem bad. Besides, we don't have a choice, do we?"

Mother continued to pray.

The two men changed the tire quickly and put the jack and the flat inside the trunk. After they finished, one of them tapped on the window. Daddy lowered the window.

"It's all done, sir." He waved and they started to walk away.

"Wait! Let me pay you something."

It took a few seconds for Daddy to roll up the window and get out of the car. He looked around and couldn't see the two men.

Puzzled, he walked to the back of the car. The new tire was on but they were gone. He looked around. He couldn't see evidence that a truck or car had stopped. He turned in the direction the two men had gone.

He saw no footprints except his own.

When he got back inside the car, he explained the strange situation to my mother.

"God answered my prayer," she said. "He sent two angels."

"Do you think they were angels? Really?"

"Christmas angels," she said. "Sent by God to help us, and they left when their job was done. In the Bible, isn't that how angels did things?"

More than forty years have passed since that Christmas and my parents have told the story many, many times. Most people believe it; a few remain skeptical.

"It doesn't matter whether you believe," my mother would answer. "We know that we had a true Christmas miracle in Connecticut when two angels watched over us by changing our flat tire in the middle of a snowstorm."

3. Our Miracle Man

Jean Matthew Hall

JERRY, MY HUSBAND, HAS DIABETES. IT IS AN INSIDIOUS DIS-ease that can destroy every major body system. Years ago it destroyed his vision. The diabetes also damaged the nerves in his hands and legs, a condition known as peripheral neuropathy.

On December 8, 2003, Jerry became ill with flulike symptoms, but he wouldn't go to the doctor. The next day he felt horrible and was even worse by December 10.

On Saturday morning he seemed to be somewhat better. We had planned to pick up my elderly mother to spend Christmas with us. Jerry insisted we should go ahead with the trip because he felt better. Besides, he assured me, he could lie down in the backseat of the car and rest during the drive. Late Saturday afternoon we headed south.

By the time we picked up my mother, Jerry felt worse than he had been in the beginning. It was late at night and I was in a dilemma. Should I take him to a strange emergency room where doctors were unfamiliar with his health problems? Should I race back home to his doctors? I prayed for wisdom and decided to head for home. I hadn't prayed that earnestly or driven that fast in my life. I made it home in record time, dropped my mother off, picked up my daughter, and raced to the Veterans Administration hospital.

We arrived at the VA Medical Center at six o'clock Sunday morning. Jerry was coughing and having difficulty breathing. He sweated profusely and was pale and weak. An EKG showed nothing suspicious. The ER doctor suspected pneumonia and admitted Jerry. Just as a precaution she sent him to ICU so he would have close observation.

I praise God for that decision.

The orderly chatted with us as the elevator slowly climbed to the third floor. He asked us to wait in the hall, and he pushed Jerry's gurney through the automatic doors into the ICU. "A doctor will be right out to talk with you," he said.

Jerry smiled and waved to us. The automatic doors slid together and he was out of our sight.

I later learned that a nurse immediately greeted Jerry then turned to pick up the paperwork. When she turned back to Jerry, he was pasty-white, his lips were blue, and his eyes had rolled up in his head. His heart had stopped. Tests later revealed that it was his second heart attack within a few days.

"Code blue ICU. Code blue ICU," sounded over the intercom system.

We heard the message, but we didn't know what the code meant and we certainly didn't think it had anything to do with Jerry. Half-a-dozen people rushed past us and into the ICU.

We watched and waited. No one told us anything.

After perhaps half an hour, a respiratory therapist came out and saw us standing in the hall. "They got him back," he said. "They're still not sure he will make it."

"What? What are you talking about?" I grabbed my daughter's hand.

"You don't know? Nobody's talked to you?"

"No one has told us—"

"I'll get a doctor." He pushed the big blue button for the automatic doors and disappeared.

Our daughter started to cry.

I tried to comfort her, but I didn't know what was going on. After perhaps three minutes, a doctor came out of the ICU.

"Your husband suffered a massive coronary." She told us they were doing everything they could, but there was little chance that he could survive. "I think you need to contact your family members immediately."

I got on the phone and started to make calls. Our son flew in from Kentucky. Jerry's brother drove from Florida. In a tiny room near the ICU we waited. Each time we saw his doctor, she paused, took my hands, and said, "Pray, Mrs. Hall. There is nothing else to do."

I was the elementary principal at a Christian school. I called my boss and he started the school's prayer chain going. Soon hundreds, perhaps thousands, of people were praying.

Jerry grew worse.

His doctor asked if we wanted him transferred to another hospital with a specialized heart team.

"Is he strong enough for the trip?"

She shook her head, placed her hand on my shoulder, and

said, "I don't believe he could make it from the floor to the helicopter alive. I have to ask, though, because the decision is yours."

I shook my head. "Keep him here."

She left us.

We prayed.

Jerry grew weaker.

December 18 was the night of our annual Christmas concert at the school where I taught. For years, the concert had been my responsibility. In my absence my wonderful staff members kept things on track, encouraged me, and prayed for my family.

They practiced and prayed while Jerry lay suspended between life and death. Friends later told me that the children sang their best that night. About eight thirty, the concert ended. Our administrator, who was my boss and friend, stood and explained to everyone about Jerry's desperate condition. He asked them to join him in praying for a miracle.

A hush came over the group as he prayed aloud. The three hundred and fifty children and adults stood for prayer. A few children cried softly. Parents and grandparents stood and prayed for God's mercy. Staff members tried to comfort children in the choir. Several people dropped to their knees to intercede for Jerry. A wave of sobs rippled through the crowd.

About ten o'clock that night a nurse came to the door of the waiting room. I climbed over our son's six-foot frame asleep on the floor, and went out into the silent hallway to talk to her.

"I don't know what's happening, but his vital signs are getting steadily better."

"He's better?"

"He regained consciousness and he's agitated by the ventilator now."

Thankful to God for sparing him, tears flowed down my cheeks.

"I thought maybe he might calm down if he heard your voice." She led me into the CCU and to his bedside.

I spoke softly to Jerry. I tried to explain what had happened. He blinked several times and pointed to the ventilator tube taped to his mouth.

Within twenty-four hours Jerry was off the ventilator and gaining strength. We spent Christmas Day in another VA hospital awaiting a quadruple bypass, but by Easter Jerry had recovered fully.

His doctor still shakes her head each time she sees us. "It is a miracle, Mrs. Hall. That's the only explanation." She turns to Jerry and says, "You should not be here now. You are our miracle man."

Today Jerry's heart is stronger and healthier than it has been for years. He praises God for answering the prayers of our friends and family, and the children in that school.

God gave us a miracle—a Christmas miracle. It was the greatest gift we could have received. Jerry is still around and we agree with his doctor, he's our miracle man.

4. Miracle of the Nativity

Tracy Ruckman

DECEMBER THAT YEAR APPEARED BLEAK. AS A NEWLY SIN-gle parent of two small boys, I worked two jobs to pay our bills. At times, it seemed I earned just enough salary to pay the babysitter, with nothing left over for the basics.

Then it got worse.

In the first week of December, the owners of the store where I worked full time decided to focus their energies on their parent store in another town, and planned to close ours within a few days. The same week I received my notice, I had a disagreement with the editor of the paper where I worked my second job. He wanted me to report a false story. When I refused, he forced me to resign.

In one week's time, I lost two jobs—both just before Christmas.

I spent most of my time seeking other jobs, and tried to keep life as normal as possible for the children. The dreary weather matched my mood, and I struggled to stay upbeat for my kids. Their world—my world—depended on me, and I seemed to be failing miserably.

On December 12, I came home from one of my final days at

work to find a black trash bag hanging on my front door. I shifted the baby to one arm, and with the other, cautiously lifted the bag from the handle. "Stay back," I yelled at my older son. I had no idea what was inside.

I put the baby down and carefully peeked inside. I laughed at my silliness. Inside was a tiny, gaily wrapped package. We pushed through the door, and I settled the boys on the sofa. "Okay, just sit there and we'll see what this is." I pulled out a package about the size of my hand. A note taped to the box read: OPEN NOW.

I tore off the ribbon and paper and opened the box.

When I revealed the gift hidden in layers of tissue paper, Zach laughed, Jonathan said, "Mooooo," and I stared.

A cow? A ceramic cow? What did that mean?

There was no note explaining the ceramic cow.

Later that evening, I called some of my friends and asked if they had given us the cow. No one confessed, but they thought the whole story was rather amusing.

We put the cow on the table and went to bed.

The next morning, there was another trash bag hanging on our door. This time, the note said DAY 2—OPEN NOW. It was a donkey.

An excited Zach rushed to the door the third morning, ready to add to the barnyard collection. Nothing was there, but later that evening his monitoring of the door paid off because we un-wrapped a sheep.

The next morning, a shepherd boy arrived and that's when I

figured out what was going on. "Twelve days of Christmas," I said aloud.

That was exactly right. Each day, for the twelve days before Christmas, we received one piece of a beautiful nativity set and it included a stable. The anticipation of each day's arrival seemed to perk us up a bit, and it caused my own focus on the season, and on our lives, to change.

On Christmas Eve, baby Jesus arrived, and our crèche was complete.

Our special gift that year was a turning point for all of us, and we knew God was with us. We enjoyed that nativity for many years.

I found work—one job that paid better than the two previous positions.

But that's not the end of the story.

Seven years later, the boys and I moved to another state to get a fresh start. We faced other trials, too. My father and my grandmother had both been diagnosed with cancer, and their deaths were imminent. "Only months, possibly weeks away," the doctors told us. We moved into my grandmother's house. She gave us her house and moved into my father's house where my sister, who lived next door, could care for them both. Once again, we began to rebuild our lives.

When Thanksgiving arrived that year, I thought of the hardships we had gone through. If we hadn't had my grandmother's house to move into, we would have become homeless. I seemed to creep through the activities of each day. Our circumstances brought to mind that other Christmas years before. We no longer had our nativity set. We couldn't afford to hire a trailer to move everything, so that was one of the items we left. At Christmas I realized how deeply I missed it.

My godly grandmother died on December 2. I felt her loss to the depth of my being. But I knew she was in heaven, and God carried us through the pain and the tears, and comforted our hearts.

A week after her funeral, I climbed into the attic, looking for possible Christmas decorations. I didn't really feel like putting out anything, but the boys were still young, and it was important for us to honor Jesus' birthday, regardless of our circumstances.

The attic was small, hardly big enough to stand in. It looked as if no one had been up there for years. But there were several boxes, so I explored each one.

When I opened the last dusty one, tucked in a far corner, and saw what appeared to be Christmas things, I closed it and hauled it back down the steps. I set the box on the sofa in front of me and reopened it.

As I unpacked the first piece, tears filled my eyes. I pulled out the objects one by one. By the time the box was empty, I sobbed uncontrollably.

In my hands were all the pieces of a nativity set—identical to the one I'd left behind. I pulled out the familiar cow, the donkey, the sheep and shepherd boy, and the precious baby Jesus. Even the stable was the same.

God was with us. That may sound strange, but the comfort

of that crèche made me aware of the love of God for my family and me.

Two days after Christmas, my dad died. That was even harder than the death of my grandmother. Friends and family have asked us how we got through that difficult time. I have only one answer: God was with us.

Now, twelve years since that Christmas, and nineteen since we first received the nativity, I still don't know the identity of the giver. But God used that gift to give us something more—he made his presence known to us, both with the first nativity set and then again with my grandmother's.

That simple crèche made Christmas a reality—twice. Both times I was able to turn my focus away from my life and remember the message of Christmas. Jesus had come into the world and had nothing, not even a bed on which to sleep. By comparison, I had so much.

My treasured nativity scene is an annual Christmas reminder of the meaning of the season. God is with us.

5. Hungry at Christmas

Geni J. White

AT THE HOUSE WHERE WE GREW UP, CHRISTMAS WASN'T bright or jolly. Although we six children made and exchanged small presents, we didn't have fancy gifts piled high under our tree. After Christmas vacation, our school friends bragged about what they had received. This year I'd have to avoid any conversation about presents.

In my younger years, our maternal grandfather mailed each of his grandchildren one present and for the family a peck of oranges. We wouldn't get anything from him this year. The previous Christmas he said he could no longer afford presents for so many children.

I was fourteen when the next Christmas came. Along with my brothers and sister, I anticipated a bleak celebration. Nevertheless, we trimmed a small evergreen that we chopped down near the Missouri River. We decorated the tree with newspaper chains, along with strands of alternating wild rose hips and homegrown popped corn, strung on Mom's sewing thread.

That particular South Dakota winter had been brutal. Frequent blizzards kept Dad from outdoor carpentry work. He was a master at interior work, but his frequent temper outbursts lost him jobs. That winter, he couldn't even find work remodeling kitchens. Mom's stress increased as she fed six growing youngsters with little money for groceries. Discouraged, Dad spent much of his time reading magazines as he huddled in a wooden chair near our living-room stove.

Mom was often sick so she couldn't handle a paying job. Besides, she couldn't easily leave my two preschool siblings to work outside the home.

As Christmas approached, I knew how little our kitchen cupboards contained. I dreaded the coming holiday, convinced we'd have nothing to celebrate.

The previous summer Mom had canned tomatoes and cucumber pickles and stored potatoes in a bin in the basement. But the potatoes softened as they aged and didn't taste very good. Worse, only a few potatoes remained in the bin.

On a dark evening before Christmas, Mom answered a knock on our front door. Two women stepped into our thrift-shop-furnished living room. They set down a huge basket of food. We children were excited at the sight. I wondered how thin wooden slats wire-lashed together could contain such wealth. A ham. Cans of fruit. Cookies. Bread. All of that I could see sticking out of the top of the basket. *Surely even more goodies were in the bottom.*

A woman in an ankle-length fur coat extended a leather-gloved hand toward Dad. Before he could respond, she closed her palm and jerked her arm close to her side. She smiled but it looked forced to me. Her eyes flickered as she gazed around our home. I sensed her disdain. She leaned down and swept imaginary crumbs of dirt from the worn upholstery of our sofa. She brushed her gloves together as if to clean them.

I cringed in shame.

"We're doing good deeds for poor, needy people this year," the older woman said. It was obvious to me that she had brought a Christmas basket for poor families, whom she apparently despised.

Her young companion wore a fur-trimmed jacket, bright-blue ski pants, and leather boots. Hands dug deep into her pockets, the girl's gaze took in our living and dining areas. She took a few backward steps toward the door before either of my parents had time to say anything.

My father moved from his slat-backed chair by the furnace, stood tall, shoulders back—I'd never seen him without stooped shoulders. "We don't need your good deeds."

I turned toward my five younger siblings scattered around in the living room. Each of them still stared at the amazing container.

Neither of the women said anything. I'm sure the other kids' eyes, like mine, followed the action as the two visitors picked up the basket. Each grasped a wire handle and they hurriedly left the house. I watched the cookies and cans of fruit vanish into the darkness before our front door slammed against winter winds.

Our visitors had been condescending and they angered me, too. But we were hungry and they left with the food. I pushed back tears and felt deep anger at Dad. *Why was he so proud? Didn't he realize we were hungry? We needed that food.*

We knew not to protest. No one said anything after that for a long time. A dark silence dominated our house most of the evening. We cleared away the remains of supper—pickles, tomato soup, and homemade bread from nearly the last of Mom's flour. In silence my oldest brother and I washed the dishes and swept the floors.

I was almost too upset to pray, but finally I said to God, "I thought you'd take care of us. Where are you? Don't you know we're hungry?"

My mind filled with turmoil and I felt I was going to cry. I didn't want to do that in front of the others and I didn't want Dad to yell at me. Hardly aware of my actions, I stepped out onto our wooden front porch. I hadn't grabbed my winter coat and temperatures were below freezing.

In the darkness my toe stubbed against something. I fell to my knees on the icy boards. As I knelt down to feel what I had hit, I realized what it was: The women had left the basket of food just outside our door.

Stunned, I wondered what to do. *Surely this is a miracle.* I quickly repented of my anger toward God and asked God to forgive me. "You haven't forgotten us, have you?"

But what if Dad refuses the food again? What if he insists we return everything to those rich women? Or tosses the food away because of his pride and anger?

Despite the freezing winds, I ran around the house and came in through the back door and walked quietly into the kitchen. I grabbed my oldest brother and whispered, "Come."

Although coatless, he followed me outside and around to the

front porch. I told him what I had found. Together we lugged that bountiful basket to the back door. Making sure Dad couldn't see us, we brought it inside. After we shoved the treasure between the metal legs of Mom's wringer-topped laundry tub, we hid the heaped-high basket under a flour sack dish towel.

To pass the time, we set up the checkers and played. Our gaze would meet and both of us were eager to say something, but we knew we couldn't as long as Dad was there. We waited and I prayed silently.

Finally Dad trudged upstairs to go to bed. Once we heard his bedroom door close, we ran to Mom and told her what I'd found on the front porch. One minute tears flowed down her face and the next she laughed. We stashed the cans and boxes inside kitchen cupboards. To our surprise, we also found six brightly wrapped Christmas gifts. Apparently they had known who we were and how many children were in the family. We happily placed these under our rose-hips-and-paper-chain-decorated tree.

On Christmas Day, we kids promised one another that we wouldn't say anything to Dad. When he came to the table, he stared at the abundant meal.

After he had eaten, Dad asked, "Where did all this good food come from?"

We kids looked at one another, not sure what to say. Mom said, "The two women left the food basket on the porch." She took another bite of ham.

I felt myself freeze as I waited for Dad to explode.

His shoulders slumped further and then he burped. He

reached for a toothpick. "How about a second cup of coffee?" he asked Mom.

My brother and I stared at each other and smiled. Dad wasn't going to throw out the food or make us return what was left. I grinned and thought, *Thanks, God, for letting us keep our miracle basket.*

From that miracle gift I learned an important lesson about God's goodness. He knows our needs and cares for us. Because he cares, he provides.

I don't know anything about the hearts of those two women—and their attitude *was* condescending—but there must have been something good in them. God touched them and caused them to leave the basket, even though they had been rudely refused. Despite Dad's temper, God had overruled and he miraculously provided a special Christmas for our family.

6. Do You Trust Me?

Edwina Perkins

"I'M SORRY TO TELL YOU," THE DOCTOR SAID, "BUT YOU have breast cancer."

Lying on the examining table, the tears wouldn't stop. I barely felt the sting from the stitches being removed from a biopsy. My doctor gently spoke to me about treatment options. His words were lost in the torrent of emotions I experienced.

I remember only three words: "You have cancer."

I have many memories of dealing with breast cancer that I won't forget. The smell of a freshly baked German chocolate birthday cake lingered in my thoughts as I sat in a hospital room on my son Garrett's second birthday. Through sobs and tears, I sang "Happy Birthday" to him over the phone. Earlier in the day, my plan had been to finish preparing for his party.

The chemo lingering inside my body took charge of my day's activities. Instead of wearing a party hat and eating birthday cake, I sat in a sterile room. Nurses entered with surgical masks to draw blood from my uncooperative veins. In the seclusion of my hospital room, I struggled with the one question that haunted me: Would I be there for my son's third birthday?

After I came home, I tried to wash my tender scalp, but the

hair stuck to my hand as it mixed with the shampoo suds. Angrily I pulled at the remaining hair, trying to ignore the burning I had experienced for days. I felt like a sheep being sheared. The shower's hot water washed my tears and hair down the drain. Later, the tender look in my husband's eyes when he saw my bald head caused me to burst into tears again.

Not all memories of my journey with breast cancer were filled with tears, however. Garrett walked around the house in my wig and called it his hat and that memory still brings a smile to my face. He sometimes sat in my lap and rubbed my smooth head. I loved those affectionate moments.

Friends loved and embraced me in ways I never imagined. Many times I paused, in the middle of another crying siege, to thank God for those people who showed their concern for me.

At my worst moments, depression filled my thoughts. I wondered if I would live. What if I didn't survive after all the terrible pain? What would my two children do without me?

At one of my lowest points I cried out to God to help me. When I paused, I felt God ask, *Do you trust me?* It wasn't audible, but clear enough that I had no doubts God spoke.

"Of course I trust you."

Even if I call you home?

I looked at Danielle and Garrett playing together. At the time, they were four and two years old. I couldn't respond. They might not remember me if cancer took my life.

"But, Lord, they would call someone else mommy." I blinked back tears as I watched my children. "They would only know me through pictures."

Do you trust me?

"That's not fair." Angrily I shoved the dishes into the dishwasher. A glass shattered before I closed the door. Pulling out the dish rack, I stared at the broken glass. In that moment, I personalized the glass and thought how closely the fragile glass represented my life. Cancer had shattered me; God's question had left me broken.

After wrestling with the question for many days, I finally got away from everyone and got down on my knees. "I will trust you, Lord, even if it means my children will call someone else their mother. I will trust you, no matter what." As I wept, God's peace embraced me.

My treatment involved nine months of chemotherapy and radiation. Metallic-tasting food became normal to my taste buds and weight gain was an unappreciated outcome of the treatment.

"I will take you as close to death as I can to save your life," my doctor said one day as I felt the deadly chemo drugs enter my body with a coldness like that of ice in my veins. His words weren't comforting. But even in that moment, I was at peace: I had made the right decision to trust God regardless of the outcome of my treatment.

After my last chemo, I asked the question that had struggled inside me from the beginning: "Can I have more children?" I had asked the question numerous times during my chemo treatments, but no one ever answered me. At thirty-one, I was the youngest patient in their practice.

I asked the question again.

Removing his glasses, my oncologist stared at me, sighed, and said slowly. "Maybe you should consider adoption."

I turned away to hide my tears.

After my treatment ended, I struggled to know how to continue with my life. Because I would be closely monitored over the next few months to see if cancer would invade my life again, I found it hard to believe my journey with the deadly disease was over.

Two years after my treatment for breast cancer ended, I waited for another diagnosis in my doctor's office. For several months, I had endured regular doctor visits and blood tests. I was worried. Something wasn't right and I had known it for days. It was as if something new had invaded my body. *Is it cancer again?* Despite the fact that my mind raced with the possible results of my test that day, I refused to focus on negative results. I had a good doctor. He would find out what was wrong.

Do you trust me?

It was that same voice I had heard during my treatment. "Yes," I whispered to God.

For another ten minutes only the ticking of the wall clock interrupted the silence of the room. Then the office door opened and the nurse came toward me. She smiled.

"What?"

"You're pregnant."

We stared at each other. I had been told that the chemo drugs used to save my life had likely destroyed the possibility of another pregnancy.

It took only one moment for the impossible to become reality.

"I'm pregnant!" Those words were the happiest words I had spoken since my original diagnosis. I drove home in a daze. Garrett, then nearly four years old, chattered in the seat next to me. I told him my wonderful news.

We pulled into the driveway and Garrett still talked about the baby. As soon as he jumped out of the car, he raced inside the house and into the arms of his father. "Mommy's going to have a baby."

I'm sure the shock and thrill on David's face mirrored my own.

This time I wasn't facing nine months of treatment to save my life; this time I faced nine months of preparation as I waited for a birth that doctors thought couldn't happen.

"It will be a wonderful Christmas present to us," I told David.

He hugged me and smiled.

Four days after Christmas, I lay on my back with tears flowing into my ears. This year they were tears of joy. I had given birth to *twins*.

At the hospital, David and I held our miracle babies, Austin and Anderson. They were our Christmas miracle. According to the medical profession they shouldn't be here, but their loud crying shouted that they were alive and healthy.

My doctor had said giving birth after my cancer treatment was nearly impossible. Delivering *twins* after having received chemo and radiation was a miracle.

Do you trust me? I didn't hear the words at that time, but I remembered them and let them flow through my mind repeatedly. "Yes, Lord, I trusted you then; I trust you now."

Since then, David and I have watched our twins grow. Often, I stare at them and remind myself that they are wholesome, living miracles. I'm reminded that God makes the impossible possible.

Miracles at Christmas still happen. I should know: I had two.

7. Christmas in the ICU

Cindy Thomson

MY FATHER HAD HIS FIRST OPEN-HEART SURGERY AND HIS first heart attack on the same day in December. He had gone into the hospital for the surgeon to repair a blockage. During surgery he suffered a heart attack. For days afterward, he remained highly sedated. I spent much of the Christmas season that year in the hospital's intensive-care waiting room at Wright-Patterson Air Force Base in Ohio.

My father underwent surgery on December 12. All surgeries are risky, but I assumed his would go routinely. It didn't. He suffered cardiac arrest shortly after the operation began.

A nurse came to the waiting room and asked my mother to step away from the people visiting with us. From a corner of the room, I heard him say, "Your husband may not make it." I bolted from my plastic waiting-room chair and hurried over to them.

"There was a lot of damage to his heart," the nurse whispered. "He's very sick. They did CPR and open-heart massage."

My mind rushed back to an episode of the television show *ER*. I'd seen the actors portray such a procedure, and the memory of it nauseated me.

"The doctor told me to come out here and inform the spouse that the patient might not make it."

I put my arm around my mom. Our pastor walked over and joined us. After we prayed, not knowing what else to do, and still in shock, I went to the pay phone and began calling everyone in the family who wasn't already in the waiting room. My hands shook, but I didn't cry.

Hours passed slower than molasses in January—something my father used to say to me when I still lived at home. After the operation, the surgeon told us he was concerned about a stroke because of the open-heart massage they had to perform. But for now, his condition was stable; Dad was alive.

For two days they kept my father under anesthesia because of the balloon pump they'd used to assist his heart. The days and hours that followed were agonizing. When I got into the ICU, my father would answer me, but I wasn't convinced he recognized me. The medication confused him. To me, the sterile hospital cubicle felt impersonal and a little frightening.

Eventually Dad improved. I carried on meaningful conversations with him, as did other family members. The doctor told me there were complications, but not being in the medical field, I didn't understand much of the information.

The days seemed to be filled with ups and downs, sending my family members and me on an emotional roller coaster that we hadn't planned to board. His caregivers took him to the regular ward only to bring him back to ICU within hours. There was some problem involved with heart fibrillation. Most people undergoing this surgery left the ICU after a day. My father remained there almost a week.

A week before Christmas my father's heart function was still slightly lower than before surgery. The doctor said that was good for a man his age who had a heart attack on the operating table. They finally moved him out of ICU.

That day I invited my mother over for dinner. I was relieved, although I knew that heart disease wasn't curable and that he would never be completely healthy. But he would get better—that was the good news.

Finally I felt it was time to get on with life. I finished Christmas shopping and cooked dinner for my family. I'd had the proverbial tough week. Two days before Christmas, my father came home. I knew I had to accept the situation and his physical condition, unpleasant though they might be, and find peace in the knowledge that a loving God is in charge.

My father told me that his first memory after the surgery was of voices in the hallway singing Christmas carols. At that time he had no concept of the trauma he'd been through, a benefit I suppose of being heavily medicated. The nurses asked him if he saw a white light or angels when he was close to death. He said he hadn't. His first memory was of people singing Christmas carols—praises to the Creator. He believes (and so do I) that the carolers in the hallway were God's messengers to bring *him* tidings of great joy. When he awakened, he felt no pain and didn't wonder what had happened. He had heard people singing about the glory of God. That was enough for Dad.

I realized that what the angel proclaimed more than two

thousand years earlier on the night Christ was born was still relevant. "Don't be afraid . . . I bring you good news" (Luke 2:10). There are many frightening things to face in this life, but listening for the good news, the hope, and the voice of angels singing of great joy can push away the bad and enable us to hear the words my father heard as he awoke in the ICU.

8. Milton's Gift

Dianna Graveman

SOMETIMES LESSONS ARE BEST LEARNED BY EXAMPLE.

Milton and his family lived next door to our family from the time I was a small child. He and his wife, Ruth, had two children, and there were two children in our household. Our families were always very close. Through the years, we celebrated birthdays and most holidays together, including Christmas Eve.

Milton was informal, and he insisted we children call him by his first name. I never saw anybody laugh as often or as spontaneously as Milton did. It didn't matter how bad the weather was, or whether or not he'd had a bad day at work. Milton greeted me daily, as he did everyone, with a hug or a wave and a genuine smile.

When I was a moody adolescent, I sometimes puzzled over Milton's consistently good humor. How could anybody be so happy all of the time?

"Sit down and I'll tell you," my mother said to me one day.

Milton had been a nineteen-year-old soldier during World War II when the army vehicle in which he was riding ran over a mine. In the explosion, he was injured. They said it was a miracle that he survived. The army awarded him a Purple Heart. But despite a permanent hearing impairment, he was filled with gratitude just to be alive.

After the war, Milton married Ruth and began a family. One day, while his children were still young, he became ill. With no previous indications of heart disease, he suddenly developed an arrhythmia that caused cardiac arrest. He was forty years old, but his heart simply stopped beating. Doctors were able to treat him successfully, and once again, he pulled through.

"Milton is happy to wake up each morning," my mother said. "He almost lost his life twice. And twice he beat the odds. For Milton, every day is a gift."

After I grew up, our families remained close. Through the years Milton never changed. For him, every day of the year was a day in which to celebrate life.

On his sixty-fourth birthday, Milton suffered a massive stroke. Again he survived, but he lost the use of the right side of his body. He could no longer speak fluently. Milton had always loved conversation, but after that he couldn't easily communicate even his simplest wishes. His mind remained sharp, which made it frustrating for those of us who loved him. We knew he still had so many wonderful things left to say.

Once again, Milton fought back with joyful goodwill. He still had that same ready wave and spontaneous grin, and he had one good arm for hugging.

A few years after the stroke, he and Ruth moved to a retirement home. Even there, Milton found a way to spread his own brand of cheer. Every year he put on his Santa hat just before

Christmas, and with the help of his walker, made his way up and down the hallways. He knocked on doors and asked the other residents, through gestures and a few words, if they had been good girls and boys. He handed out gifts of candy and other goodies. Everybody looked forward to Santa's visit.

Early one December, my mother suffered from heart failure. Milton was ready with as many comforting words as his limited speech allowed. "Okay," he soothed. "Everything . . . okay."

As Christmas drew near, Mom slowly improved, and I began to appreciate the lesson Milton had been teaching by example: Each day *is* a treasure, regardless of the obstacles ahead.

It took time for my mother to regain her strength, but my family had been given a wondrous gift. We would all be together for the holiday.

It's unfortunate that life didn't go according to our plan. A major winter storm blew in just in time to stop our annual Christmas Eve celebration. The members of Milton's family and mine lived several miles from each other, and weather forecasters warned motorists to stay off the slippery roads.

After much deliberation, we decided we shouldn't get on the roads. We decided to phone them. It was the first Christmas Eve in many years we wouldn't be together. I was extremely disappointed and so were the others in our family.

But Milton would have none of our sadness. For him, every day was a celebration, and this holiday would be no different. "Ho . . . ho . . . ho!" came Milton's halting speech through the telephone receiver. "Love . . . you."

"I love you, too, Milton."

Then I cried. Once again he reminded me that every day truly is a gift.

Milton is no longer with us, and yet every year when the holidays roll around, I remember the miracle of his lesson—and the marvelous Christmas spirit he shared with us every day of the year.

Each year I want to shout to him, "You're right. Every day is a gift. Every day we're alive is God's miracle of love for us." I also add, "And, Milton, thank you for teaching me."

9. Three Christmas Eve Miracles

Fred W. Iverson

I STOOD AT THE WINDOW ON A BITTERLY COLD CHRISTMAS Eve in 1948. A heavy winter snow dominated the bleak landscape. I scraped a hole through the cold frost on the window. As I did so, I silently prayed for a safe trip home for my father. I was only ten years old, but a feeling—a sense of worry—came over me as I watched for the headlights of Dad's 1934 Ford V8.

It wasn't time for him to arrive, but I couldn't push away the nagging fear that something had happened or might happen to him. Please, dear God, I prayed silently, take care of my dad.

Dad worked on a construction job one hundred and twenty miles away. Whenever he could, he came home on weekends. This trip, of course, would be special: He would be home for Christmas.

The thought of having Dad home with us gave me a warm feeling, and yet I couldn't pull myself away from the window. I prayed again for his safety.

Why am I worried? He's made this trip many times. He's a safe driver.

Many of the highways in South Dakota are long, straight roads with little traffic. Like everyone else we knew, Dad drove fast on those roads, especially when he came home to his family.

What if . . . ? I stopped myself from thinking that way. "Bring Dad home safely," I prayed softly as I continued to stare out the window. "Please."

After what seemed like a long wait, the car's headlights finally glowed through my hole in the frost on the window. "Thank you, God," I cried as I waited for him to come into the house.

I felt such relief and wondered why I had been so worried. I didn't know when he walked into the house that I had experienced three wonderful Christmas miracles.

Years later, Dad told me what had happened. His Ford V8 was fast and, eager to get home to be with us, he pushed for top speed. Normally that wouldn't have made a difference. But something significant happened that night.

At ninety miles an hour, his Ford hit a patch of black ice. He lost control and the car left the road. Dad ducked under the dash so the rolling car wouldn't crush him. The car continued to bounce through a cornfield. To Dad's amazement, it remained upright—all four wheels remained on the ground. His hands shook for a few minutes as he realized that he was unhurt.

He sat up, put his hands on the steering wheel, and his foot pressed the accelerator. Everything felt normal. Cautiously, he drove the car across the corn stubble and shallow snow to the road. He drove a little slower the rest of the way home.

That year marked one of the best Christmases I had as a kid. That was a night of miracles, but like many significant things in life, we don't grasp their impact until later. I hadn't been any superspiritual person; I was only a kid who loved his father and wanted him home. As I watched for Dad, I had started to worry. That worry turned into action to pray for his safety.

God nudged me to pray for Dad's safety and I did. Wasn't it a miracle that God would "speak" to a ten-year-old boy? Ordinarily, I wouldn't have prayed for his safety. As a kid, I assumed he'd be all right.

There was a second miracle: Dad's powerful experience of divine protection. He drove at ninety miles an hour, hit black ice, and ended up in a cornfield. Wasn't it a miracle that Dad wasn't hurt or the car damaged?

But the third miracle continues to encourage me even today. God answered my prayer. That may not sound like much to many because most of us adults assume we pray and God intervenes. But I was young, and a kid who knew little about God and didn't understand divine intervention.

Can you imagine how that event has helped to shape my life? God listened to me. I had my personal miracle of the Lord responding to my cries. That was the beginning. I learned I could ask God to help. I've reasoned many times since then that if God listened to a ten-year-old kid, God would surely listen to me as I continued to mature.

Yes, it was a special night to remember the birth of Jesus. It was also a special night of Christmas Eve miracles.

10. Homeless at Christmas

Sandy Cathcart

"I CAN'T SET FOOT IN THAT HOUSE ONE MORE TIME," I TOLD God. It was Christmas Eve, 1979. "I desperately need a miracle." I sat in the passenger seat of our family car and between sobs I told God that he had done what he said he wouldn't do: He brought more trouble into my life than I could handle.

The first blow happened two days before Thanksgiving when our house in the country burned to the ground. We learned years later that our son, Clay, who was five years old then, had played with a friend's cigarette lighter and caused the fire.

I tried to put out the blaze. When it was obvious I couldn't, I gathered our children and ran from the flames. We had no phone and my husband, Cat, had taken our only car to work.

We hiked a quarter of a mile away to the home of our nearest neighbor. No one was home, so I pried open the window so my younger son could get inside and use their telephone. By the time the Forest Service unit arrived, the fire had destroyed our home. We had nothing but a smoldering mass of rubble.

We had no insurance and less than ten dollars in the bank. My husband's boss insisted we come and stay with him and his family. We appreciated his kindness, but a family of six taking in a family of seven had to be a big inconvenience. In preparation for Christmas, they had decorated the house and a pile of presents for one another lay under the tree. Because of having no insurance, my husband's paycheck had to go toward finding a new home. I felt bad that we couldn't buy our children a single gift.

God seemed far away.

We had just returned from the latest rejection. Four children sat in the backseat. None of them said a word and allowed me to cry. Our oldest daughter, Michelle, cried along with me. I reached for my youngest child and held her in my arms. I wiped my eyes on her blanket and tried to force a smile to assure her that everyone was all right and we would be all right. It didn't work: I couldn't stop crying.

Cat sat beside me and stared across the barren landscape of leafless trees and frozen sod.

My heart felt as frozen as the cold scene. I had been so sure that God would come through for us and provide a house. Instead, we had been homeless for a month, unable to find anyone who would rent to a family with five children and two dogs. We had searched for a house to buy, but without a sizable down payment it seemed impossible.

Just then, our host opened the door and called out, "Sandy! Your mom's on the phone!"

"I can't talk to her now," I whispered to Cat.

"What should I tell her?"

I shook my head.

Cat sighed and stepped out of the car. He hated to talk on the phone. At that moment, I was so caught up in my own pain I couldn't focus on Cat's discomfort.

We stayed in the car and he went into the house. Not more than three minutes later he came back, got inside the car, and turned on the ignition. He backed out of the driveway.

"Where are we going?" I asked.

"Your grandmother is in the hospital. Your parents are ready to leave so they can spend time with her."

Until then I thought I had reached bottom. Only minutes earlier I had grumbled to God because he had given me more than I could handle. Now he had given me even more.

"Don't you love me?" I asked God. I had no sisters or brothers, and I deeply loved my grandmother, who lived more than a thousand miles away. *Will you take her as well?* I couldn't stop crying. I wept all the way to the adult trailer park where my parents lived in a mobile home.

Mama met us at the door. She held out a bulky white envelope.

I pulled out several sheets of paper with signatures on them.

"It's a petition signed by all my neighbors. They've agreed you can stay in our mobile home while we're gone."

New tears came, but this time they were mixed with surprise and joy.

"We're leaving within the hour. You can move in now."

I don't know which surprised me more—that the neighbors

would allow us to stay in an adult-only park, that my shy mother had mustered the courage to take the petition door to door, or that God answered my plea to not have to stay another night with our friends.

I grabbed Mama and gave her a tearful hug.

"That's not everything." She pointed to a small, already decorated, and lighted Christmas tree. Under the tree were presents for each of us. She pulled out a white envelope that had been stuck between the branches. As she handed it to me, she said, "It's from your Uncle Bill."

Uncle Bill had sent us one hundred dollars and a note. "This money is to be used to buy Christmas gifts for your children and not for anything else." I read the words two or three times before I handed it to Cat.

I fell into the nearest chair. My body wracked with sobs and I asked God to forgive me. "You haven't brought me more than I could take. Forgive me for doubting and for giving up."

God hadn't given me more than I could handle. While I was sinking deeper into despair, God had already provided. I thanked God for being faithful even when I was faithless.

While my parents waited, Cat and I sped downtown to take advantage of Christmas Eve specials. Never before or since have I had so much fun picking out gifts for our children.

Christmas morning we heard a knock, but when we opened the door no one was there. Looking down, I saw that someone had brought several bags of food. Inside we found a turkey, cans of pumpkin, sweet potatoes, and cornmeal. I had food for Christmas and enough left for almost a week.

The memory of God's faithfulness carried us through four more months of homelessness. At times, I still broke down, but I never again accused God of being unfaithful. Despite every setback, I never again doubted his love for me and my family.

11. The Day God Laughed

Marcia Lee Laycock

WE HAD BEEN TOLD IT WOULDN'T HAPPEN. AFTER FIVE years without conceiving, my husband and I had decided to pursue adoption. The social worker who interviewed us said, "You're certainly good candidates, but it would be advisable to find out why you cannot have a child together."

From our home in Yukon my husband, Spence, and I traveled to Vancouver, British Columbia, and underwent a series of tests at a large hospital. After all the tests were completed, the doctors still couldn't give us a definitive reason. One of them said, "It is extremely unlikely that you will ever have a child together. Pursuing an adoption is likely your best option."

My heart broke at hearing those words. We had prayed often and hard for a child. We couldn't understand why God wouldn't let us have a baby.

We tried to resign ourselves to that reality.

Although I hid my deep sadness from others, I found it almost unbearable. No one knew how much I wanted a baby of my own, but the clues were there. I felt angry much of the time. I believed God was punishing me for things that happened when I was a child. I vacillated between hating God and convincing myself he didn't exist. The bitterness poured into all aspects of my life. I couldn't see myself, of course, but I'm sure I wasn't very nice to be around.

Until the day God laughed.

It happened on the road to Mayo, Yukon. I was on my way to visit a friend, glad to get away from the question my husband had frequently asked: "Do you believe in God?" I tried to evade the question whenever possible. Some days I did. I was glad to get away and have an excuse not to go with him to the tiny mission church he had begun attending.

As I drove, I was determined not to think about God, religion, or any of the baffling ideas my husband continued to bring up. But no matter what I tried to focus on, my mind wouldn't rest. The question of God's existence and what he had to do with me wouldn't go away.

In desperation, I pulled my vehicle into a lookout point above the Stewart River. The beautiful river valley stretched out below, but I barely saw it. My mind in turmoil, I challenged God to do something to prove to me that he existed. I asked God to forgive me and admitted I was confused. I was more than a little frightened that my husband's decision to involve himself with religion could destroy our marriage.

I realized how foolish I was, talking to a God I had all but convinced myself did not exist. At that point something happened that I haven't been able to describe adequately.

I heard laughter.

Yes, it was inside my head and it wasn't audible, but it was laughter. Immediately I thought of a grandfather chuckling. I heard these words: "But I love you anyway."

The laughter and the words were more real than if my own grandfather had sat beside me in the car and spoken.

Am I going insane? Has the stress finally pushed me over the edge? Am I now hearing voices?

"This is crazy," I said aloud. I pulled onto the road, stomped on the gas pedal of my truck, turned the radio up as loud as it would go, and drove rapidly toward my friend's home.

Our visit turned out to be more discussion of spiritual things, which I hadn't expected and didn't want. But I kept my composure.

By the time I returned home I was determined not to pursue Christianity. I would humor my husband's interest in it, but I wouldn't be drawn into religion.

Besides, I wasn't feeling well. For several days, I had suffered from an odd strain of flu. Each morning when I awakened, I felt nauseated but after lying in bed for a while, I could get up and my appetite suddenly became immense. I wanted a huge breakfast.

About the seventh day of this flu, I figured it out: *I was pregnant.*

That reality reminded me that I had challenged God to do just that—to show me a sign. The child growing in my womb was his answer and the proof of his love. It was a miracle of life.

First God laughed at me. Then he gave me the desire of my heart. She was born on November 30, 1982.

On December 10, we braved the frigid Yukon winter to attend the Christmas pageant at the small mission church where my husband attended faithfully. By then I had also become a believer and one of the members.

We went there with our ten-day-old baby, Kate. The service wouldn't be a grand production, but that was all right. The building was a tiny and dilapidated hall. They sang carols a cappella because they had no pianist. Six or seven children, dressed in bathrobes with kitchen towels wrapped around their heads walked up to the platform. The backdrop was made of cardboard stars covered in tinfoil.

But it didn't matter. It was a special time for me. I saw everything in a new way. The tinfoil stars glittered more brightly than a chandelier. The carols were as harmonious as though sung by angels, and the children made the story come alive. I watched as if that pageant had been my first.

As I listened to the Christmas story, it was as if I heard it for the first time. I had just been given the desire of my heart, the evidence of a miracle, the precious gift of a child of my own.

"See what you have to look forward to now?" whispered a friend behind me and pointed to the children.

I nodded. Yes, I saw. I saw a future filled with the knowledge there is peace without measure, grace without limit, and love without conditions. I saw a future suddenly bright because I believed the Christmas story.

A tiny baby, whose sole purpose was to die for me and all others, had been born in Bethlehem more than two thousand years ago. I saw that the reality of the Christ of Christmas is still intimately involved in our lives here on earth. Although the church was just a hall, the music less than perfect, and the costumes homemade, the story is exquisite.

God had laughed at me, but he hadn't forsaken me. He gave me the one great desire of my heart. I hugged my daughter even closer.

12. The Gift

Pam Bostwick

WHERE ARE MY GLASSES? I WONDERED AS I SEARCHED through the mountains of last-minute Christmas purchases scattered on the kitchen table.

Agitated, I emptied my purse. I was sure the glasses had been with me when I left the house that morning. In my hurry to hit a dozen crowded stores and wait in long checkout lines, they could have dropped out anywhere.

The doorbell startled me. Gayle opened the door and called, "Are you ready to go?"

"Go where?" Then I remembered. "Oh! No, not today! I'd forgotten about our plans to volunteer at the care center."

"You sound frazzled."

"I've lost my glasses." I tried to keep the panic out of my voice. "I can't see clearly and I can't read a thing when I don't have them." I was visually impaired and I felt helpless in public without them.

We searched, but didn't find my glasses. Gayle finally said, "We're going to be late."

"But my glasses," I said. "I can't go without them—"

"They're counting on you at the center."

She was right and I knew it. "I guess I'll go, although trying to see those dear people probably won't make me happy today." Before she could tell me I was overreacting about the glasses, I said, "It's more than that. This Christmas I feel hassled and overwhelmed."

Carols played on the car radio as Gayle drove. The music made my head pound, but I didn't feel I could ask her to turn off the Christmas music. "It's not the season to be jolly for me," was the only complaint I made.

Wisely, Gayle didn't answer.

When we reached the nursing home, one of the directors, Mrs. Murphy, gave me another reason to be depressed. "I'm glad you were here on Grace's eightieth birthday." She hesitated before her voice softened. "Grace died a few days ago. I thought you'd want to know."

Numbly I took in her words. Grace was gone and it further saddened me. The last time I saw her, I became acutely aware of her need to feel loved. When I got ready to leave, I hugged Grace and she clung to me. I wondered if she had known it would be our last good-bye.

I wheeled the residents from their rooms to the multipurpose area. My elderly friends comforted me over the loss of Grace. I thanked them and forced a smile, but her death made this one of the worst Christmas seasons I had ever known.

Decorations of holly and lights adorned the halls. The festive atmosphere did little to lift my mood. I had work to do, so I pushed aside my misery. These people were hungry and expected a good Christmas dinner. I attempted to enjoy the stories and music, but inside I felt restless and despondent.

The residents captured the simplicity and meaning of the holiday. When they sang with the choir, their voices rang out with laughter and love. The messages of peace sank deep within my soul. I needed them. I was where I belonged. So why then did I feel despair? They had so little, yet they appreciated little things, even a simple song.

After the program, Mrs. Murphy approached me. "Can you come with me? I'd like you to meet Linda. She's recently been sent here for rehab after a car accident. I think you're what she needs."

Reluctantly, I followed Mrs. Murphy to a darkened room at the end of the hall. She opened the blinds before she said, "There's someone I want you to meet."

"I don't want to see anybody," Linda said. "Not anybody."

I felt tempted to leave. Linda didn't want company any more than I desired to visit.

I forced a smile. "Hi, I'm Pam. I'll sit here awhile so you won't be alone."

"I'm used to being alone."

"Why is that?"

"I can't go home for Christmas."

I stroked her hair, which lay in a braid on the pillow. "I'm not much in the spirit of the season either. How sad you can't spend the holidays with your family."

"I was in traction for ages. I'm still in a lot of pain."

"I haven't been through what you have, but I've had a bad day. I lost my glasses. I'm only partially sighted, and I see even less without them."

"Gosh, we all have our problems." That was the first time her voice showed any softness.

I began to rub her shoulders, which were tight with fatigue, but seemed to relax with my touch. "Sometimes it helps to talk."

"If I bring up the accident, everybody acts uneasy and distraught. They say there'll be time later to discuss Ritchie's death, when I'm better."

"What happened?"

"It was a nightmare: the weaving car . . . screaming tires . . . burning rubber, the explosion, shattering glass . . . a drunk driver." Linda's voice rose. "It's not fair that Ritchie died so young in such a senseless way."

I hugged Linda while the sobbing shook her body. "I don't want to keep it inside that my big strong brother is gone. But it hurts so much. He can't joke around anymore, or give me advice or give me those nice bear hugs. He was full of life. I feel frozen, unable to move. I miss him so much."

"I'm sorry." I embraced her again and I also cried. "It's not the same thing, but I found out today that my friend Grace died. I feel lost and empty, too."

Linda wiped her eyes. "The hurt doesn't go away, does it?"

I shook my head.

"It does seem bearable when someone listens and understands though." Despite her tear-streaked face, she smiled.

"That must have been so wonderful to be loved by your big brother."

"I adored him. He was like—like a father as much as a brother."

The sound of carolers interrupted us. We listened as they sang "Silent Night," before their voices floated down the corridor.

"That was Ritchie's favorite carol. Every Christmas Eve, his voice boomed that song through the house. This year he won't sing it, and I'm stuck here. I wonder if God has forgotten me."

"Maybe God has sent you the song to remind you that Ritchie hasn't forgotten you, and that he is here with you now?"

"I hadn't thought about that, but I guess we have our memories." After a few more minutes, she said, "You've been good for me. I feel uplifted from our talk," and she pushed the nurse's buzzer. "They've been trying to get me up and going. I'm ready to do that now."

God had tried all day to bless me with the tranquility of his son's birth. I finally had ears to hear and I received a renewal of my faith in that room.

A nurse bustled into the room. "I heard you call. I came running now that there's a sign of life here."

"This is where the action is!" Linda tried to make it sound sarcastic, but it didn't work. She made an effort to sit up. "The doctor says he wants to get me moving on my legs. I'm ready to get up and get at it."

"What happened in here?" The nurse turned to me.

I shrugged. "Sounds like Linda is that much closer to going home." I smiled at both of them.

"Our rehab lady is here today," the nurse said. "I'll bring her down here." She left to get her.

Linda stared out the window. "I can't wait to leave this dreary center. The lonely, desolate circumstances of these people here pulls me into thinking I'll never improve. I have to keep reminding myself: I have hope, I will heal. Most of these people won't ever leave here, will they?" She stared out the window as if in reflection. "Maybe there's something I can do for them."

"I have a hunch there's plenty you can do to make a difference for them and cheer up this drab place."

"I could paint Christmas cards and decorate rooms with homemade ornaments." Her tone brightened. "I still have my hands and I'll be able to push myself around in a wheelchair to visit with some of the residents."

I smiled as I listened to the change that had come over her.

After she threw out several ideas, she paused, stared at me, and squeezed my hand. "Thank you. It's funny what you'll tell a stranger."

"I believe we began as strangers and have become friends."

Just then Gayle opened the door and she must have heard us talking. "You're the one who didn't want to come."

"But now I'm glad I did."

"You better hurry back, Pam," Linda called. After I promised I would, she called out, "Hope you find your glasses."

"Oh, I will." As I said those words, I realized the glasses were no longer important. God had given me a special Christmas gift. Linda had been God's gift to me. Just being with her made me realize how blessed I was to be able to encourage another person.

At my house, I retraced my steps, calling each place I had been and asking about my glasses. "It's in your hands, Lord," I said.

The next day, a second miracle happened. Someone at the restaurant where I'd grabbed a snack called. "We combed this place last night and your glasses weren't here. I don't know how it happened, but they turned up today."

But I knew.

13. Black Shoes for Christmas

Cecil Murphey

Two days before Christmas, Mom still hadn't said anything about our presents. At the sink I soaped a plate and rinsed it. "Elmer's getting a dog for Christmas."

Instead of taking the plate, Mom shook her head slowly. She didn't look at me, but even at nine years old, I sensed something wasn't right. Before I could ask what was wrong, she removed her glasses and polished them with the bottom of her apron. "We won't have any Christmas this year."

"Dad's working again," I said. He had been sick for three months but had gone back to work after Thanksgiving.

"There . . . isn't . . . any . . . money." She burst into tears and buried her head in her apron. Dad's first check had gone for rent, groceries, and gas for his car.

Mom fumbled inside her wallet, and emptied its contents on the kitchen table. A dime and three pennies rolled across the checkered oilcloth. "That's all the money until after Christmas when your dad gets paid again."

"God will give us what we ask for," I said. "See, Mrs. Garbie [my Sunday school teacher] says we should pray."

"I . . . have . . . prayed," she said as fresh tears came.

The answer seemed simple to me. "Mom, you have to tell God *exactly* what you want, and then you'll get what you ask for."

"Sometimes we don't get what we want."

"My teacher said we would and she knows. So you'd better make a list and pray."

Probably to humor me, Mom pulled a stub of a pencil from her purse and sharpened it with a paring knife. On the back of a calendar she wrote our names and listed a toy for my two brothers. "Now what do you want?"

"New shoes," I said. Even at that age, I was the practical kid in the family. "And I want black ones."

"What if you get something else?"

"No, I'm going to get black ones." Our school principal wore black shoes with metal taps on the heels. When he walked down the hallway, I liked to listen to the clicking of his footsteps. I didn't know anybody whose shoes shone so brightly. I wanted a pair the same color. "I'm going to ask for black and that's what God will give me. Mrs. Garbie said so."

The sole of my brown shoes had come loose on the right foot, and I finally cut it off. By the next day I had worn a hole through the inner sole and my socks as well. I stuck pieces of cardboard into the bottom, but they wore through after walking in the wet snow.

I didn't know much about praying, but I told God about the principal's black shoes and that I wanted a pair like his. "They don't have to be that nice. I just need shoes. And God, just to be sure you know, I want to tell you again, I want *black*."

When Christmas morning came, we all gathered in the living room as soon as we finished our oatmeal. We didn't have a tree, but Mom had hung red and green strips of crepe paper over the windows. Her eyes filled with tears, she handed my two younger brothers and me a small bag of candy. Mom began to sing "Silent Night." When she was sad, she often sang hymns.

My dad didn't say anything. He kept his head down while he tied and retied his shoes.

Just then a Salvation Army truck pulled up in front. My brother Mel ran to the door. He brought a fat, smiling man into our living room, who handed Dad three large boxes.

"We didn't ask for help," Mom said.

"Somebody told us," he said. At the door, he smiled again and said, "Maybe it was God."

"It was!" I yelled. "God told them!"

My brothers had fun pulling out boxes and trying to figure out who they were for. I waited for my shoes. Mel handed me a box of checkers, but I wasn't much interested; I only wanted my shoes.

Soon the boxes were empty. "Where are my shoes?"

"I guess there aren't any," Mom said.

"I asked for black shoes. Why didn't I get them?" I couldn't cry in front of my dad, so I stomped my foot.

"Sometimes God just doesn't give us—"

"Maybe he took them to the wrong house." Tears stung my eyes, but I wasn't going to give in.

"Everything doesn't work out the way we want," Mom said and stroked my shoulder.

"God promised!" And as far as I was concerned, I had done what Mrs. Garbie told me and God hadn't kept his promise. I had been so certain about the shoes, and now I didn't know what to do. "I'll wait," I said. "Maybe the truck will come back soon."

No matter how often I ran to the window and looked outside, the Salvation Army truck didn't come back. No one else brought gifts.

Mom cooked a Christmas dinner of chicken, cranberries, and sweet potatoes from the food they gave us. I didn't want food; I just wanted my shoes. Every time I heard a car, I hurried to the window.

Finally, just before dark, I walked to the end of our snow-covered street to see my friend Chuck Baldwin. Since I wasn't going to get my shoes, I didn't want to be home where I'd keep thinking about them.

Each year for Christmas, Chuck's father bought rebuilt shoes for the family—shoes brought in for repair and never claimed. I went into their house and took off my shoes because my feet were cold and my right foot was soaking wet. I rubbed my toes to get them warm again.

"Look," his mother said and pointed to my shoes.

"I didn't mean to make a mess," I said, embarrassed about my tracks on her linoleum floor.

They whispered something to each other, and Mrs. Baldwin went into another room. When she came out, she handed me a pair of shoes. "If you can wear them, they're yours."

I stared at them. They were black! Although rebuilt, they

had been polished so nicely they looked new. I held them up to my face and smelled the polish. "They'll fit all right!" Those were *my* shoes and I knew it.

"We got them for Chuck, but they're too small," she said, "and the man won't take them back." She said Chuck could wear his brother's shoes from the previous year.

My left foot slid right in. I put a cold, wet right foot into the other. I tied the shoes, stood up, and walked around. They were a perfect fit, just as I knew they would be.

Minutes later I raced into our house. "Look, Mom! God gave me the shoes after all!"

Mom looked up and smiled. It was the brightest smile I'd seen on her face in months. Tears followed her smile.

I walked around the room to show off my shoes. "See, just what I asked for. And God even gave me the right color."

At that age I didn't know much about God and stopped attending Sunday school shortly afterward. But I never forgot about the black shoes at Christmas. Years later when I reached crises in my life, that simple miracle became one of the factors that enabled me to open myself to God.

14. A Ruined Christmas Eve

Sunny Marie Hackman

SOMETIMES, CHRISTMAS WAS A BIT MORE THAN I COULD tolerate. With kids at home, kids in college, married kids, grand-kids, and extended family I want to shout, "Stop! Stop the bus! I want off at Thanksgiving."

All my family lives in the same town, and my in-laws come to visit us or we go to their house. It gets hectic because of everything that goes on. My kids have expectations, my family has expectations, and I have expectations. When I was little, I had been content with the large brown box that contained my present. After taking out my simple gift, it was fun to curl up inside it and listen to the sounds of Christmas.

It had been a long time since I was satisfied with a box or the sounds of Christmas.

My most memorable hectic Christmas was one of those times when I felt pulled and pushed from one end of the city to another. All three of our kids promised that they would be home on Christmas Eve for our special Christmas celebration. That particular night was mine to dictate, and I would make everything perfect. It was the one event I looked forward to and that kept me focused instead of running in various directions.

I had a clever idea: We would have a progressive dinner. We would start at my mother's house and have clam chowder and spinach salad. While there, we'd spend time with her before we hurried on to our house. I would serve Perfection Prime Rib made from the recipe in the *Colorado Cache Cookbook*, page 153, as well as mashed potatoes and gravy, and green beans with mushroom soup and onion crunchies on top. We would open the gifts at our house before we went to my aunt's house for dessert. My aunt doesn't bake, but she buys only the very best, so the dessert would be delicious.

Our son, Vic, planned to arrive by bus that evening, and was scheduled to join us somewhere between soup, salad, and the main dish. After he called, Dad and Grandpa would run down to the bus depot and pick him up. I figured that would take twenty minutes, tops. I could live with that minor inconvenience.

The evening went smoothly. We had been to my mother's house and had barely walked in through the front door of our house. The phone was ringing.

"This is perfect timing. We just got in," I told Vic. "Dad and Grandpa will be right down to get you." I was excited that he was exactly on time. "It's so good to hear your voice."

Then he shocked me.

"What? Let me get this straight," I said, trying not to let my voice betray my objection. "You want to know if it is all right to bring home some guy for dinner—someone who hasn't seen his family for five years?"

Vic went into an explanation, but I hardly listened.

"I guess it will be okay," I said after he paused, "but this is not what I had planned." I'm sure he caught the irritation in my voice. *You have ruined the perfect Christmas Eve.*

Doesn't Vic realize how much this evening means to me? I'm his mother and I've worked for days to get everything ready. We certainly couldn't open our gifts with a stranger present.

My plans for the evening would come to a crash. After all my planning and fretting, our son had ruined the perfectly planned Christmas Eve dinner.

I couldn't say too much because I had always tried to model Christian hospitality for my children; however, when I did show hospitality, it was at *my* convenience. The inclusion of a stranger *wasn't* convenient. When was that person going to leave? What if he decided to stay for the entire Christmas vacation? For the next fifteen minutes I fretted and reminded myself to be gracious and friendly.

After they walked through the front door, I tried to be friendly and make conversation, but the atmosphere was strained. We sat down at the dining-room table. Everyone tried to make the best of it, but I sensed our guest knew that I wished he hadn't come. Vic did give me some relief when he told me the young man's parents would be there in a couple of hours to pick him up.

Our guest ate several helpings of everything, including the prime rib. He seemed to enjoy the dinner. After we finished the meal, I casually asked him if he played the piano or guitar.

"As a matter of fact I do," he said. He picked up the guitar in the corner of the room. He played Christmas carols, and we sang with his accompaniment. It was pleasant to sing the carols. After all, it was Christmas. The atmosphere grew peaceful after a few songs.

Our guest put down the guitar and walked over to the piano. He began to play and sing the most beautiful medley of "Amazing Grace" and "Jesus Loves Me" that I had ever heard. When he finished the atmosphere was reverent.

My daughter broke the silence. "That was so beautiful. Can you do that song again?"

"No, I can't," he said and stared straight at me. "That was my gift to you."

After that, I felt like a different person. Something had changed me. I couldn't explain what happened, but I knew I was different. Instead of resenting him, I hated it when he left us. I wanted to cry out, "Not yet. Not yet."

That had been the intruder who ruined my beautifully planned Christmas Eve. I needed my plans upset.

Painfully, I looked at myself and realized that I had been so focused on me, my wants, my convenience, and my plans that I wasn't ready for surprises or interruptions.

That young man's quiet and simple giving of himself taught me the true meaning of Christmas. It's not in the planning activities and controlling people that makes the season special. In receiving others as they are and the gifts of themselves we can grasp a sense of God's unspeakable gift of love to us.

"Oh, dear God, I'm so sorry," I cried that night. I asked God to forgive me and to change me. And God has done just that. I can honestly say that Christmas at my house has always been different since the angel came for dinner. That ruined Christmas Eve remains the most special one.

15. The Greater Miracle

Shawnelle Eliasen

LAST YEAR, I STILL GRIEVED FROM MY MISCARRIAGE. AT OUR church's Christmas pageant, just seeing baby Jesus had broken my heart.

Lonny and I sat in a back pew. Our church sanctuary had been transformed to a stable with hay bales, fresh evergreen boughs, and candles. "Silent Night," a cappella, drifted heavenward. Soft light fell on the manger, and the holy family appeared. My friend Susan played Mary. Her long brown hair touched the bundle in her arms. She gazed at her own newborn child.

I sat in the pew with empty arms. There would be no swaddled babe for me. *Why did you choose to take our baby, Lord?*

God didn't answer, and I knew he wouldn't. I cried.

Lonny put his arms around my shoulders and whispered, "Do you want to go home?"

I didn't answer, but gazed straight ahead. My heart felt like a rock.

The blow of miscarriage seemed especially brutal because we had prayed for that baby for so long. The petition became a family dedication. Each night our two boys dropped to their knees at the foot of their double bed.

"God, please let us have a baby," Logan prayed.

"Yeah, we'd take good care of him," Grant usually added before they dove under the covers.

We had prayed for a baby for four and a half years.

At last, it seemed that God had answered our prayers.

One summer evening, after the boys were tucked in, I pulled Lonny by the hand. We went down the stairs, through the house, and out the back door to the porch swing.

"What's going on?"

The cicadas sang and the swing whined, but I couldn't speak at first. I stared at the summer sky and ran my finger over the bandage on my arm. "I went for a blood test today," I said. "We're going to have a baby."

Lonny's eyes filled with tears. He pulled me close, and I wept. "Thank you, God," he whispered.

Two months later, we lost that baby. I felt betrayed and abandoned by God and bitterness crept into my soul. How could he have allowed me to conceive the baby for whom we had prayed so long and then take it away? Hadn't he seen the bowed heads and folded hands of my little boys?

To make my pain worse, a number of women at our church had babies. There seemed an endless entourage of pink booties and blue knit caps. *God, I trusted you and dedicated my family to you. Why did you do this to me?*

I couldn't push away the sadness, and it seemed to worsen every day. One afternoon, I felt more sad than usual. I needed to be alone. I tried to stay in my bedroom, but my boys tracked me down. As I tried to read, they raced Hot Wheels over the arms of the wing chair, across my lap, and down my legs. I needed some space. I pushed the cars away and stood to shove the window open.

The air stabbed at my lungs. I closed my eyes and let the cold hit my face. After some time, I opened my eyes. In our neighbor's driveway, a young woman got out of a car. She opened the rear door and lifted a blue bundle from an infant seat. As she walked up the sidewalk, she clutched the baby to her chest. She bent her head to kiss a small cheek. Tiny legs kicked from under the blanket.

I broke down. Deep cries came from the pit of my stomach and filled the room. Lonny ran into the room.

"What's going on? Stop it!" I told him what I saw. "You're scaring the boys." He grabbed our sons and took them outside.

"You are cruel, God! I know that you see my pain. Yet you parade babies in front of me. I told you that I'd raise my family for you. Do you hear me? *For you!*" I wailed until my throat felt raw. I dropped to the floor and curled up into a fetal position and sobbed. I had never felt so alone.

I didn't break down again. The crisis had passed, but I still hadn't forgiven God. Weeks later, I learned that I hadn't been alone at all. Even as I accused God of abandoning me, another son was being formed inside my womb.

"Forgive me," I prayed. "Forgive me."

Months later, I lay in a hospital bed, fighting through the fog of medication. I'd had general anesthetic for the C-section. Sleep pulled at me, but my spirit urged me to awaken.

Today was miracle day: I would get to meet my son.

I opened my eyes. A small Christmas tree sat on the bedside table of my hospital room. The branches drooped with Popsicle-stick sleds and pipe cleaner wreaths. Two poinsettias decorated the windowsill. Our CD player in the far corner softly played Christmas music with a gentle dink of Christmas bells.

A nurse came in. Her rubber soles padded to my bed, and she checked my vitals. I heard the rumble before I saw the bassinet. Lonny pushed it and his grin was new-daddy proud. He bent down and kissed my forehead. "Are you ready to meet our son?"

I whispered, "Yes."

Lonny turned and lifted the swaddled bundle closer. Samuel's face could've been porcelain. Dark lashes fringed crescent eyes. His downy black hair swept out from under a Christmas red cap.

My hands were tied in tubes, but God's grace was so near that I wanted to reach out to touch it with my fingers.

Christmas bells rang softly on the CD. Lonny held our son, and I saw God's grace in giving us our long-prayed-for son.

Oh, God, please forgive me. You wanted to comfort me, and I pushed you away. I blamed you and I turned from you. But you blessed me anyway. I thought that Samuel was the miracle, Lord, but I see the greater miracle. It is your grace.

I lifted my arms to receive my newborn son. And I lifted my spirit to receive God's grace.

16. A Small Christmas Miracle

Beverly Hill McKinney

A FEW DAYS BEFORE CHRISTMAS, I SAT IN MY FAVORITE chair quietly reading. A loud, shattering crash at my patio window startled me. I dropped my book and rushed to the window. I looked around my backyard, but I saw nothing.

Everything seemed peaceful. A light snowfall blanketed the yard. Although a slight breeze blew through the small trees, I could see nothing out of place. Despite the accumulation of ice, I couldn't see anything broken.

Just then, I looked down on the mat just outside the glass door. Crumpled in a tiny heap was a hummingbird. His head had dropped down on the mat and his wings curled toward his body. The sun reflected off his bright, fluorescent green feathers and as his head lowered, flaming red feathers showed from his head.

Did this bird cause such a crash? His eyes closed, his head drooped, his wings drew inward, and he seemed to be giving up.

I don't know why, but I felt such a strong impulse to pray for that tiny bird. As a teacher, I thought of the prayer requests from children over the years who asked the Lord to heal their pets. I made a point of telling the children that if the same God who created the universe was mindful of us as individuals, he would want to make us happy and be mindful of our pets as well. After their many simple childlike prayers, they often came back to class and told us that their pets had been restored to good health.

First, I paused to thank God for his beautiful creation, especially during the Christmas season. Then I earnestly prayed that God would touch the injured bird that lay lifeless on my welcome mat. I stood there for several minutes, just watching.

After perhaps three minutes, the wings slowly stretched back out from the still-silent body. One wing unfurled gradually, followed by the other one. The red head slowly tilted upward. The eyes opened, but the bird didn't move.

I decided to move back from the glass door so I wouldn't startle the creature. Just then without a shake or shiver, the bird stood up and flew across the yard toward our large cherry tree. The sun glistened off the tiny wings, and within seconds the hummingbird was gone.

Joy rose in me as I realized that I had witnessed the healing hand of God in my presence. Many might say it was coincidence that such a thing happened—and that's all right. I believe differently. I'm convinced that God is mindful not only of human creation, but he loves all his creatures as well.

As I stood there, marveling at the Christmas miracle, I thought of my own words. Through the years I had said to children at our church, "Nothing is too hard for our Heavenly Father." I prayed with the simple, childlike faith I had observed in my students.

They had taught me well.

I stood quietly for several minutes. Christmas was near and I had gotten caught up in activities and preparation for the big day. I had also missed small miracles that constantly happened around me. For the next few days, I realized that I had become so busy with the less important aspects of Christmas and had forgotten the purpose of the season.

It took the injury of a hummingbird to make me ponder the real meaning of this most special time of the year. Small miracles are around us, we need only to watch for them. As we value the small miracles, we can rejoice over the greatest of God's miracles—one that took place in an obscure town more than two thousand years ago.

17. Breakfast with Santa

Claudia Dadara

RED SOCKS UNDER THE TABLE ACROSS FROM ME GRABBED my attention that Christmas Eve morning as I ate breakfast with two friends at a local restaurant. After I spotted the red socks, I stared at the elderly man who wore them. He sat by himself. He wore a gray suit and dark shoes and those socks seemed totally out of place.

I couldn't seem to divert my attention from him. I'm not sure why, but I had such a strong desire to talk to him. Not wanting to be rude to the people with whom I ate, I made them aware of the man with the magnetic-colored socks. "I'd like to talk to him. He seems so alone."

I hoped my friends would encourage me to go over to his table, but they didn't. Something about seeing a person eat alone, particularly the elderly, often tugs at my heart. I tried to ignore him, but I kept being drawn back to stare at his red socks. "I'm going over," I said to my friends. They smiled indulgently and continued to eat.

"Excuse me, sir." He didn't respond so I spoke a little louder. "Excuse me, sir."

His head turned to me and he smiled. "Yes?"

"I wanted to tell you that I love your red Christmas socks."

"Oh, thank you." His voice raised an octave. "I'm on my way home to put on the rest of my red suit."

"So, you're Santa Claus?"

He smiled and his face lit up. He told me his name was Ralph. I sat down beside him as he told me his story. After his wife died, he felt lonely without her, almost as if he had no purpose in living. Late one afternoon, a rainstorm came, and a loud thump on his roof caught his attention. He reasoned it might be nothing or it could have done some serious damage to the roof.

After the rain was gone, he got out a ladder and climbed up. A large tree limb had fallen on his roof. The slippery rungs of the ladder made it impossible to get a good grip on the tree branch. He pulled, his feet slipped, and he plunged to the ground.

Unable to move, he lay there. Fresh rain mixed with blood soaked his clothes. He stayed there for two hours until a neighbor spotted him. The man rushed Ralph to the hospital.

They put eighteen stitches in Ralph's head. Because he was unable to walk and had no one at home to care for him, the hospital transferred him to the rehab center. "It was terrible for me. I was sick and lonely. I was afraid I would die in there."

My sympathy went out to Ralph as he told me the rest of his story.

"I promised God that if I got out of that place, I'd visit the area rehab centers and nursing homes to spread joy." Tears filled his eyes and he said, "So that's what I do."

After we chatted a few more minutes, he pulled out a small,

insulated blue bag and placed it on the table. He unzipped the bag and passed it over to me. It contained a variety of miniature candy bars, including my favorite, Snickers. The shiny wrappers seemed to twinkle in the reflected restaurant's light.

"Go ahead. Help yourself."

I chose two Snickers and sat at the table and ate them. I remembered my friends, so I called them over. I introduced Ralph, the man with the red socks, to my friends as Santa Claus. "After he finishes breakfast, he'll be on his way to rehab centers to spread the joy associated with Christmas."

They smiled and we chatted with him for several minutes. Ralph made it clear that he wasn't just a Santa. He visited those places all through the year.

When we finally left, I thought, *Today is Christmas Eve. I've had the privilege of having breakfast with the real Santa named Ralph.*

That was enough of a Christmas miracle for me.

18. All I Want for Christmas

Madeleine Kuderick

MY SON, BEN, HAD ONLY ONE WISH FOR CHRISTMAS: HE wanted to be able to read. We had tried everything for him, including tutoring, reading therapies, and phonics infusion. Nothing worked.

A month before Christmas, I watched my son's painful reading process. He winced as he tried to unscramble, what for him, were pages of jagged, jumbled letters. As I watched I thought, a note to Santa might be a nice diversion.

I pulled a sheet of blank paper from the bureau and suggested it. He shook his head. Even the simple task of writing a list of anything frustrated my son.

After I nudged him a little, he said, with tears flowing down his face, "I have a secret wish. It's the only thing I want for Christmas."

"What's that?"

"All I want for Christmas is to be able to read."

Then I cried.

Although his words had been heart-wrenching to hear, my son's wish inspired me. That night, I prayed for an end to his long struggle with dyslexia. Unable to sleep, I penned rhyming verses, thinking that I would send them with our Christmas cards that year.

Only days before Christmas, my ten-year-old son did something utterly amazing. He read his first book cover to cover. That may not sound like much of an achievement in an age where children are learning to read and write before they learn to tie their shoes. But it was for him and for me.

I can't explain it and I often say his ability to read sneaked up on me. Looking back, I realize that his gradual reading improvement showed in several ways. He no longer reversed letters such as *b* for *d*. His misreading of simple words happened less often. He no longer read *on* when he meant *no* or *of* when the word was *off*.

In December, I watched in awe as my prayers were answered and my son's wish came true. He began to read. Slowly at first, but each day seeming to be a little more fluent. Daily reading sessions began to spark his imagination instead of inciting his frustration. Soon, he had favorite characters and authors. He was reading entire books. His level of self-confidence grew as his reading level improved.

For our Christmas letter, I sent the poem I had written weeks earlier. As my son discovered the joy of reading, people around the country read the message of my son's simple wish. They hung the card in teachers' lounges and on refrigerator doors. They passed it across coffee tables and backyard fences. Many called to share how deeply the words had touched them.

That's how our Christmas miracle reached beyond our own home and one boy's dream to read. For a single wondrous time in December, many people were reminded that miracles can be found in the smallest of things. My son helped them to remember that nothing should be taken for granted. But most important, he showed them that all things are possible.

This is the poem inspired by my son's Christmas wish:

Can you reab what I reab?
"Go ahead," his mamma said. "Santa needs to know."
She pushed the blank sheet toward him, soft and smooth and slow.
His little fist came crashing down with all its tiny might.
"I guess I'll just get nothing then, if I have to write!"
His mother paused a moment, then held his angry hand.
"Just one word," she coached him. "St. Nick will understand."
She wrote the first half-sentence, then drew a long, blank line.
"Fill it in," she softly said, "I know you'll do just fine."

He grimaced at the paper and crumpled up his face.
He wanted it so perfect, no scribbles to erase.
But his earnest little sentence grew wild as a weed.
"All I want for Christmas is to nrael how to reab."

"Nrael how to reab?" his mamma asked aloud.
Then something swelled inside her, feeling sadly proud.
No Xboxes or GI Joes or Legos topped this list.
The simple act of reading was the gift that this boy missed.

"I want to read like Jacob and spell like Mary Jo.
I want my of to not say off, my on to not say no.

I want my backward ds to flip. I'm done with broken sounds!
I want St. Nick to help me stop from thinking upside down."

"Nrael how to reab!" Ma cheered. "Why that's no lump of coal!"
So she mailed his hopeful letter to Santa's old North Pole.
"You'll swim among the stars," Ma said, "with silver eels to hook!
There's no escape more magical then the wormhole of a book."

And so the boy slept restlessly, dreaming of those words,
watching backward 7s fly away like birds.
He threw a wand to Harry and opened Wardrobes, too.
"Come on back!" Tom Sawyer cried, "When your dream comes true."

But when the Kringle read it, his face grew grave indeed.
There was no toy in Wonderland to teach a boy to read.
He tugged on his long whiskers and crinkled up his brow.
"Toy or not," he said at last. "We'll make it true somehow."

So on the eve of Christmas, he sent his reindeer fleet
to ask the midnight stars to blow their dust down to his feet.
The elves were tap, tap, tapping like tiny ticking clocks,
their mallets molding stardust into shimmering smooth rocks.

"This stone is for his teacher," Claus said with a grin.
"Whenever there's a struggle, her creativity will win.
Whenever there is hopelessness, her praise will build him up.
And in his thirst for knowledge, she'll fill his golden cup.

"This stone's for his parents," Claus said, quite amazed.
"It's grooved to soak up worries from a thousand anxious days.
It's glowing with their hopes and dreams, with endless rays of joy,
for each new sound and syllable awaiting their bright boy.

"This one's for the boy himself," Claus said without a doubt.
"It pushes all his fears aside and lets his strength come out.
It magnifies his giftedness: his heart; his hands; his mind.
And with his newfound confidence, the words he's sure to find."

Then with a wink, the sleigh took flight. The winds began to
*   billow.*
Toys were fluffed and stockings stuffed, and stones tucked 'neath
*   each pillow.*
And under sleeping heads that night, the Hope began to seed,
*That this would be the year, in fact, the boy would learn to read.**

My son received his wish; I received my answer to prayer.
Both of us rejoice in the miracle that took place that Christmas.

* First published in *Reading Today* 26 (3) (December 2008/January 2009): 40.

19. Stranded in Thailand

Scati Springfield Dameij

ON DECEMBER 22, I WAS READY TO GO HOME, NEARLY EIGHT thousand miles away. I had just experienced four fabulous, once-in-a-lifetime weeks in Thailand.

On my last day, I stopped in front of the beggar I had passed every day. Perched in his battered wheelchair, he resembled a stone Buddha. His eyes stared straight ahead. Instead of knees, two stumps stuck out a few inches past the wheelchair's seat. Healed balls of skin capped his amputated stubs.

I dropped all my coins into his metal cup. *That's probably more money than he receives in a month.* I felt right about doing it.

After I made a few impulsive purchases, I received more change. A paraplegic man teetered on the filthy curb's edge between the busy street and crowded sidewalk. Seeming to be alive only from the waist up, his shriveled, lifeless legs appeared as wooden as his worn crutches. I dropped all my remaining coins into his cup, our gaze locked—two people from different worlds. His radiant smile and joyful eyes conveyed a silent thanks.

I returned to the hotel and bargained hard with the taxi

driver to avoid being overcharged for the ride to Bangkok International Airport. As we sped along the freeway, he said, "I miss my daughter. She live five hours away. To make money, I buy taxi and work in Bangkok. The cost of gas hurt my business." I understood his pain—insufficient finances or time with your children. Too often in the past I had worried if I would have enough money to fill my tank with gas to drive to work.

By the time I had recited my entire Thai vocabulary, we were nearly to the airport. "You speak Thai good. How much you pay?"

"Just as we agreed, three hundred baht."

His eyes registered disappointment, but he said nothing. He blinked and regained his upbeat composure. "You single woman. I take good care of you."

At the Bangkok International Airport, the taxi driver unloaded and stacked my slippery plastic suitcases onto a baggage cart. I pressed all my currency into his hand—five hundred baht, plus eight American dollars.

I was broke, but I didn't need any money until I returned home. After passing through security, I checked into China Airlines and received my boarding pass. At the exit immigration window, I explained, "I need my one thousand four hundred baht VAT [tourist value-added tax] refund to pay the five hundred baht exit tax."

"The VAT Refund Office is in the departure lounge," the woman said. "You cannot pass through immigration without paying." Despite my protests, she shook her head and turned to the next person in line.

That's when I realized my problem. I was stranded because I couldn't get to the departure lounge. I had no money. Not one cent. *God, please don't let me miss my plane. It's Christmas. I just want to get home to my family. Please, please, Lord, show me what to do.*

My plane was scheduled to take off in two hours and I lacked five hundred baht (fifteen dollars) to clear immigration so I could board the aircraft. *How will I get home? Why had I been so stupid and given away the rest of my money? Why hadn't I thought about a possible and unexpected expense? Why had I given my money to those two beggars and the taxi driver?*

Tears ran down my face. I returned to China Airlines to ask for help. "Please excuse me," I said, "I need help. I don't know what to do." The airline employee, who took my ticket, was checking in a passenger with distinct Thai features—large round eyes, rounded nose, full lips, and sculpted cheekbones. Most Thais stand five foot four. She was six feet tall, maybe taller.

I explained my situation to the attendant, "If you can just let me go through to the departure lounge, I'll get the money and—"

"Traveling is stressful," the tall woman said. Before I could say anything more, she handed me a bill. "Take this."

I stared at my hand. She had given me one thousand baht. That was more than enough. "Thank you. I'll pay you back on the other side of immigration."

"Do not be concerned about it."

"But I am. I will pay you back."

As I slid five hundred baht under the immigration window

and was cleared to go into the departure lounge, I silently prayed, *Thank you, Lord, for hearing my prayer and providing for me. Now I can get home to celebrate your son's birth with my own sons.*

The immigration officer at the door inspected my passport. "You overstayed your visa. That will cost an extra two hundred baht for each day." She did allow me to collect my refund from the VAT Refund Office, which paid the remaining overstay fees.

I entered the departure area and realized I hadn't eaten. It might be a long time before they served the meals on the plane. I still had a few coins in my purse after paying at immigration. It wasn't enough money to repay the woman but it was enough for me to buy a sandwich, chips, and an icy watermelon drink. While I ate, I looked for the tall woman. I wanted to get her address so I could mail the money to her.

By the time I finished my food, I still hadn't seen her. I walked to the other waiting lounges. I looked carefully. Twice. I even went into the restrooms.

I didn't see the tall woman.

I decided she must already be on the plane so I went ahead and boarded. I walked down the two aisles and looked at every face.

She wasn't there.

I sat down and pondered what had just happened. I had given freely to those who had no way to repay—just as Jesus told us to do. The tall woman had given just as freely to me and I couldn't find the stranger to repay her.

Tears of gratitude slid down my cheeks. The God who gave his son as an infant at Christmas was still giving to the world. I was across the world from my family, but not unnoticed. Even before reaching America, I had already received a special Christmas present.

20. Miracle on the Train

Violet Moore

I WANTED TO BUY MYSELF A CHRISTMAS GIFT. MY TWIN SISter and I rode the Metro Light Rail to downtown Sacramento during the holiday shopping season. We planned to browse through the mall and walk to historic Old Sacramento before we returned on the early-afternoon train.

After we spent an hour of going from store to store on a cold, rainy day, my sister had purchased one gift for a grandchild, but I still hadn't bought my own present. The aroma of food enticed us to stop at a small eatery. Large pots of soup cooked on open flames while teen workers prepared specialty sandwiches. They seemed in no rush and appeared unconcerned that hungry shoppers hurried in and wanted to finish quickly.

We found a table away from the cold and sipped hot coffee while we waited for our order. After an incredibly long wait, the hot soup was delivered to our table. I lifted the disposable container from the tray. The lid wasn't secured properly and hot soup streamed down my left arm. I gritted my teeth and moaned from the pain of the hot liquid on my arm. I wiped my arm with napkins while my sister asked for help. None of the employees responded.

A nearby customer showed me to the washroom. I ran streams of cold water on my arm and I groaned, "Lord, help me. I can't be hurt two weeks before Christmas." My words sounded like a complaint more than a plea for divine intervention.

The customer returned with tiny ice cubes in a clear bag and left again in search of a store manager. Holding the makeshift ice pack on my arm, I walked slowly back to my table. I was acutely conscious of sympathetic looks from other customers.

"Where is the first aid station in this mall?" I asked the young man who had taken our food order.

"There is none." His tone sounded indifferent.

I asked him for burn spray or antiseptic cream, something to soothe my burning arm and hand. The pain seemed intolerable.

"We used it all and haven't replaced it," he said. He walked away and returned a few minutes later with a well-used first aid kit. He opened it and I saw that it was almost empty. Worse, it contained nothing for burns.

"I need medical assistance," I said. I explained that I had ridden the Metro train to the mall and needed transportation to an emergency medical clinic.

"The mall doesn't have any kind of transportation."

"Not even when there are accidents?"

He shook his head. He didn't know the location of the nearest medical treatment facility. "You're on your own."

My arm burned and he seemed indifferent to my situation. "Give me an injury report form for emergency treatment," I said. "I'll ride the train back to the station where our car is parked and go to a clinic near there."

"Okay," he said.

Grimacing from the pain, I said, "The medical facility will bill you later."

It seemed like a long time before the young man returned, and I hurt so badly, every second seemed long. A mall-management supervisor was with him.

"That's a severe burn," the woman said as she stared at my red, swollen arm. She gently cleaned my arm with an alcohol wipe and applied a second wipe from a package labeled "For Stings." She wrapped my arm with a gauze bandage from my elbow to my wrist. "That's for protection on the train." She copied information from my identification, took incident statements from my sister and me, and left to copy the completed form.

After another interminable wait, she handed me the finished documents. My sister and I left and walked several blocks through cold, drizzling rain to the train stop. The pain seemed to intensify as we hurried down the street.

The train was crowded, noisy, and cold. I sat next to the window, guarding my arm. My sister sat on the aisle to keep commuters from bumping me. Among the crowds, a tall dark woman wearing a bold plaid suit and spiked heels walked from car to car touching each seat and shouting loudly above the noise, "Every knee shall bow and every tongue shall confess that Jesus is Lord!" She stomped her stiletto heels alternating with a loud "Hallelujah! Thank you, Jesus!" as she approached us.

A startled man quickly moved away after she touched his seat. Others pretended not to notice her and some seemed offended. She touched our seat, but I didn't look at her.

I was in too much pain to say little more than how much I admired her courage to exercise her right of freedom of speech on a public transit system.

The passenger near me shrugged at my remarks. He said he was from New York City where strange passengers were routine.

When the tall woman exited the train at the next station, I heard her continuous chant in the same rhythm while she walked outside and continued crying out the same words among passengers boarding the train.

Despite my pain, there seemed to be something melodiously soothing in her ecstatic rantings.

A security guard stared at her for perhaps a full minute before he entered our car to check tickets. Exhausted, I closed my eyes, trying to block out the burning pain. I could hear her chants until the train pulled away.

After several stops, we arrived at our destination and walked to the car parked nearby. As we drove to a nearby medical facility I realized that the burning sensation had stopped. I felt no pain. Slowly and gently I unwound the bandage to look at my injured arm. What I saw stunned me.

My arm was normal. There was no redness. No swelling. No blisters. No scars. The only reminders of the severe burns were the bandage, soup on my clothes, and the completed injury report form. *Could it have been the antiseptic wipe?* Doubtful, I answered myself. It was only alcohol rubbed on a small area. *Could it have been vibrations from the faith of the chanting woman?* Perhaps.

I stopped trying to discover the source of the cure; instead, I relished the power of the Christmas spirit. I smiled, grateful that my destination was home rather than an emergency clinic. I didn't need to do any shopping for myself: This miracle was my own special Christmas gift.

21. Holy Ham at Christmas

Celeste Coleman with Jane Rumph

THE GRAVEL CRUNCHED UNDER MY TIRES AS I PULLED INTO the parking lot off Fair Oaks Avenue. Through the dusty windshield, the little church didn't look like much. Late-afternoon shadows changed the white stucco to a shade of chalky gray. But I knew the drab exterior hid a gold mine of goodwill.

Carrying my pot of black-eyed peas and neck bones, I headed for the fellowship hall. "Merry Christmas, Pastor Joe," I called as I passed his office.

"Hello, Celeste."

Pastor Joe and his wife had a special vision. When they first came to minister at our church, they didn't see the limitations of a small facility in a run-down neighborhood. Instead they envisioned reaching out to dozens of families who struggled with hunger and homelessness. They looked with God's eyes and believed that they could feed and house eighty-six people there every night. The Lord blessed their vision, and the Fair Oaks Family Shelter was born.

My Sunday school class, along with several groups from other churches, committed to provide dinner for the shelter once a month. I'd been surprised when Paul Peterson from our class asked me to coordinate the outreach. Although many others had more training and resources than I, Paul insisted that God had given me a special gift for that kind of ministry.

"Mmm, that smells good," I said as I entered the kitchen. Two current residents prepared corn bread and a rice dish. Other class members had already dropped off their contributions to the meal. I'd asked Paul to bring the ham, and others supplied coleslaw, canned sweet potatoes, cake, and ice cream.

Peeking into the fellowship hall where people had gathered, I was delighted to see that someone had made festive centerpieces that added color to each table. Next door in the sanctuary, the couples, single parents, and children would sleep tonight—two days before Christmas.

I enjoyed ministering to those families because I loved them and understood what they experienced in being homeless. As I mashed the sweet potatoes I reflected on my first encounter with the Gospel on a day I had no food for my three kids. I went to my neighbors in the apartment building where I lived, invited them over for a party, and asked each to bring something for a big stew.

That's how I got my children fed, and that's when the man who brought the onions told me about a God who loves us. It was a long time before I finally started going to church, but I never forgot the simple but compelling message that God will provide if we trust in him.

After I did get involved with a congregation, I realized that God didn't change my circumstances so much as he changed my outlook. Time after time I would stand at the brink of crisis. But instead of panicking, I had someone to whom I could turn.

God always came through and provided for me—often with some seemingly miraculous provisions—even one time when I was homeless myself. My children and I lived in a motel for three weeks until God helped us find a place to live.

"Excuse me, Celeste." The woman making the rice reached across me for a serving spoon and pulled me back to the present. I focused on my work and put the sweet potatoes into the oven to brown the marshmallow topping. While I waited, I surveyed the kitchen and decided everything was ready.

"It's five thirty," I announced. "Let's put the dishes on the tables."

As the food went out, a nagging feeling crept over me that something was missing. *The ham!*

I turned to one of the shelter residents. "Did a man come by earlier to drop off a ham?"

"It's in the refrigerator."

I yanked open the fridge door, and saw nothing. Scanning the shelves again, I spotted a canned ham. *One ham—an eight-pound canned ham.*

I picked it up and a wave of dread passed over me. "Are there more?"

"No, I guess that's the only one."

We stared at the can silently. I hadn't told Paul that I wanted a freshly cooked *twenty-pound ham*. There was no time—or money—to buy more. The other dishes were hot and ready, and eighty-six hungry people smelled the good things and would soon become restless if we delayed.

Lord, help us, I prayed silently as I went to work. I took out the ham and set it on the cutting board. With the ham in one hand and a knife in the other, I prayed silently, *You're going to have to do something about this ham.*

I started to slice, and as I did I felt my spirit calming. I cut the ham crossways and down the middle. The other women arranged the slices on metal pie trays to put them under the broiler for a quick warming.

I stared at the trays I had prepared and thought, *I'd better cut them again.* I cut the ham slices in half and the trays went into the oven, one batch after another.

Finally we carried all the ham to the dinner tables. The guests eagerly helped themselves to the feast, and we sat down to join them.

A little later I spotted the first empty plates. People leaned back with satisfied smiles. Scanning the tables, I spotted one untouched tray of ham slices. *How could that be?*

"Did everybody get a piece of ham?"

"A piece?" someone answered. "I think everybody had two or three pieces of ham."

"Two or three pieces?" I repeated blankly. I stared at the leftovers as intently as I had stared at the small can earlier.

Then I understood: God had provided. He had taken that little eight-pound canned ham and transformed it to meet the needs of eighty-six people plus the workers. What I had disdained became a multiplied blessing in God's hands.

Most of the people we fed had no idea what happened. After we cleaned up, we went into the sanctuary. Pastor Joe led in singing a carol, and my eyes rested on the nativity scene. Two thousand years ago, I realized, most people had no idea of the miracle that had taken place in Bethlehem. A baby in a manger didn't look like much. But wrapped in swaddling clothes lay the world's savior. As I joined in the singing, I blinked back tears.

I had been present when God performed a miracle. I felt blessed and greatly privileged.

Loading the car later with my empty pot, I looked back at the little church; the lights in its windows burned brightly against the dark night. Inside, its precious guests prepared to bed down in the warmth of its shelter.

"Merry Christmas," I murmured to no one in particular. Yes. It would be a merry, wonderful Christmas once again.

22. Always a Christmas Tree

Pamela J. McCann

OUR FAMILY OF SIX FACED FINANCIAL STRAIN MANY TIMES over the years, but we always had a tree at Christmas. It's not that we were materialistic or felt it wasn't Christmas without one. For us, a tree symbolized a special part of our family life.

Twice during my growing-up years, we almost didn't have a tree. The first time was in 1963. That year everything looked bleak for us. It was the poorest period I remember in my childhood. My father's furniture store went bankrupt and our car was repossessed. The telephone company even took away our phone.

Despite the lack of money, we were determined to celebrate Christmas. "We have to have a tree," my thirteen-year-old brother, Bob, said. He took his axe and went into the woods to cut one down and bring it home.

He chopped down a large blue spruce. But once he had it down, he realized it was too big for him to carry or to drag home. After thinking about it, he decided to cut down a smaller spruce, one about six feet tall. When Bob brought it into the house, he did so with pride, even though it was scrawny, misshapen, and sickly looking.

But it *was* a Christmas tree. Even though it was less than perfect, Mom said, "Doesn't the tree smell wonderful? That's why a live tree is so much better than an artificial one. It fills the house with that amazing scent."

Ten years later, we faced another bad holiday season. My brother and two sisters had married and I was still in high school and lived at home. Again, my parents faced financial problems and they seemed even worse by the middle of December. The local price for a tree was twenty dollars.

With tears in her eyes, Mom said, "We can't afford to spend the money. We need to buy groceries." I knew we would have a wonderful Christmas dinner just as we did every year.

Not to have the aroma of a spruce or a pine in the house didn't mean that much to me, but Mom's disappointment saddened me. I wished I had the money to buy one.

A few days before Christmas vacation, I sat in Ms. Maxwell's Spanish class. She had brought a beautifully decorated four-foot live Scotch pine into the classroom. As I stared at it, I wondered what she'd do with it once school let out for the holidays. I didn't concentrate well on my Spanish that day because I continued to think about the Scotch pine.

After the bell rang and the others left the room, I went up to Ms. Maxwell and asked, "What will become of the tree when the school closes for the holidays?"

"The janitor will take care of it."

Before I could think about my words, I blurted out, "Could I have it for my parents? We won't have one this year and it will mean so much—"

"Of course you may have it," she said. "But how can you get it on the bus?"

"Oh, that's not a problem. I'm a walker."

At the end of school on Friday, which was the beginning of our vacation period, I took off Ms. Maxwell's decorations, picked up the Scotch pine, put it on my shoulder, and left the school. I probably should have felt tired from the load, but this seemed like such a special gift to me.

Snow started to fall as I walked slightly more than a mile to our home. I felt a sense of God's presence and was excited that I could do something nice for my parents. As I came near the house, Mom stood at the window. It was a moment of perfect beauty for me to see her framed there with snow gently landing on the sill. Just then Mom saw me and rushed out of the house to embrace me. Together we brought in Ms. Maxwell's gift. Mom's smile was the brightest and warmest I had seen in weeks.

I thought of the words from the Bible, even though I didn't know where they were located: "But my God shall supply all your need according to his riches in glory by Christ Jesus" (Philippians 4:19 NKJV).

Those were the two difficult years. After that, we had a Christmas tree every year. Once all of us were gone, my parents' financial burden lessened. We came home as often as we could and each year the tree in the living room was the focus. I suppose that's why Christmas trees are so important to me. I associate them with this special, wonderful time of the year.

My brother Bob died in 1981 and Mom passed away in 1996.

Although Pop suffered a stroke in 2003, he was still alive in 2007. Just before Thanksgiving, while he was in a nursing home, Pop became quite ill. The doctor said it was double pneumonia. Aware that my father was weakening, I slept on a recliner next to his bed.

I was awakened early the next morning with such shortness of breath that I had to get out of the recliner and move around before I could breathe properly. *Something doesn't smell quite right*, I thought. I sniffed, and the scent of blue spruce filled the room. I smiled and thought, *Yes, just like the scraggly spruce Bob brought in 1963.*

There's no Christmas tree in this room, I thought. Perhaps the delightful fragrance came from the hallway. I opened the door and stepped into the hallway, but there was no scent there.

I went back into the room and again inhaled, and the blue spruce aroma was stronger than ever. That's when I understood. I can't explain except I *knew*—I knew God used that fragrance to send me a message. He wanted to prepare me for Pop's leaving. A deep sense of peace came over me.

That night my father died peacefully.

For me, smelling the aroma from the blue spruce also meant something else: Mom was close by. As Pop passed from this life, I believe with all my heart that Mom was waiting to greet him.

I wanted Christmas of 2007 to be special—something to remind me and my siblings of my parents and to remember the special times we had shared in our home. For each of us, I bought an artificial miniature tree and tied little bows on the branches. I cut the bows from a white eyelet blouse that had belonged to

Mom and the rest from Pop's favorite red and green flannel shirt that he had worn frequently during the Christmas season.

To some, my story may not sound like much—but it's special to me. It's special because God spoke to me through the scent of blue spruce the morning before Pop died. I believe it was a message from heaven.

Christmas began with the miracle of a baby's birth in Bethlehem. Each year, the memory of that aromatic message reminds me that the miracle-working God still provides those little, unexpected messages of hope.

For me, the little miracle was as simple as the fragrance of a Christmas tree.

23. A Christmas Basket

Laurie Kalp

"KATIE, YOU'RE BURNING UP. WE NEED TO GET YOU TO THE doctor." I hugged my five-year-old daughter who had struggled with a cough for weeks. It had gotten steadily worse the past two days. My husband, Pete, had been up most of the previous night with her. A few times she had coughed so violently that she vomited.

Two weeks earlier we had taken her to the doctor. He put her on antibiotics, but her condition hadn't improved. On that cold, cloudy morning, she wasn't any better than she had been before my surgery. I had been home from the hospital for only a few days after my hysterectomy.

Pete rushed Katie to the doctor as I waited at home with our two young sons, Andrew and Nicholas. I watched them play in front of the Christmas tree as I thought about Christmas traditions. It was December 23, 2004, and I worried that Katie's illness might mean that she needed to be hospitalized.

After Pete and I married, we spent every Christmas Eve together and attended Mass at the cathedral as a family. After that we ate dinner at my parents' home. On Christmas Day, we woke up early and opened our presents before going to a relative's home for dinner. I had been grateful to be out of the hospital in time to celebrate with my family.

Pete called and said that chest X-rays confirmed Katie had pneumonia and a sinus infection. She would have to be admitted to the hospital immediately. While I packed a bag for Katie, I called my parents and asked them to come over to our house.

"Christmas in the hospital?" Mother asked. "A five-year-old should not have to spend Christmas in the hospital."

"It's not a choice," I said. "Katie is sick with pneumonia. She has to get better. We've tried everything at home—breathing treatments, steroids, and cough medicines and—"

Mother understood and said little as I paused from the packing. Tears gushed out. I had to wipe my eyes before I could say the most important thing. "I'm scared. Really scared."

"Your father and I will be right over. You don't need to get upset right now, either. You rest and recover from your surgery. We'll take care of things."

I hung up the phone determined to do what I could to get Katie better. I decided to put aside my pain and sit with her all night. I prayed for strength and for God's mercy on Katie. I had turned my life and my will over to God seven years earlier. Since then, God was the first one to whom I turned.

My father drove me to the hospital and my mother stayed with the boys. When I reached Katie's room on the pediatric floor I saw her lying in the bed with IVs in her arm. I said another prayer, asking for strength. I leaned over and kissed her and then sat beside her.

"I'm scared," Katie said.

"Everything will be all right." I stroked her hair. "I'm right here." My words sounded far more assuring than I felt.

Before long, Katie went to sleep, but I stayed there, keeping vigil while she slept. I prayed softly and fervently. I asked God to make her well. I also thought how lifeless and pitiful she looked. Were we doomed to have the worst Christmas ever? How could I be strong and positive for my daughter, when I felt bad myself? My body was sore and I had little strength. Would we be able to cheer her up? It seemed as if our family had been through so many hard times lately and I was tired of it.

"God, won't you give us some type of Christmas miracle? Something to brighten this situation?"

The nurses were aware that I had recently had surgery, so they joked about whether they should wheel in another bed for me. I said I'd be fine sleeping on the pullout bed.

That night was physically and emotionally painful for me. It was worse for Katie because she didn't seem to get any better. It seemed as if nurses came into the room every hour to check her temperature, give her breathing treatments, and take blood. Both of us barely slept.

The next day was Christmas Eve. Katie had improved, but she wasn't well enough to go home. As I sat beside her bed, I felt sorry for myself and for my family. I prayed from time to time and asked God to help us.

We live in southeast Texas, and to have a white Christmas rarely happens. But that year the conditions were exactly right. Snow gently covered the outside world. When Katie awakened, I pointed out the window to the snow. She excitedly watched the first snowflakes accumulate on the windowsill of her hospital room. It brought big smiles to Katie's face.

We watched the snow as we listened to carolers coming down the hall, bringing music and gifts to the sick children. To our surprise, the singers were people we knew, and they came into the room. That brightened Katie even more. Groups from several churches also stopped by to bring gift baskets for Katie and to pray with us.

It might be a different Christmas, I said to God, and one that we would never hope for, but it's still good. The wonder and the joy of the season seemed to stir my heart with peace for our family that night even though we weren't doing our usual Christmas Eve activities. We wrote Santa Claus a letter so he would know that Katie was in the hospital. When he left for the night, Pete took the letter home with him. He promised Katie he would put it by her stocking so that Santa wouldn't miss it.

On Christmas morning, Katie woke up to see that Santa had found her. He had brought several presents to her hospital room and a note to say that he wished her the best.

"It's a miracle that Santa Claus found me here," Katie said. "I didn't think he'd know where I was." Her color was better and her cough had almost disappeared.

Just then I learned we could take her home. Once home, Katie and I, pale-faced and weak, sat around the tree for our annual Christmas picture. God has truly blessed us, I thought as I smiled for the camera.

I learned an important lesson from that Christmas experience. For me, the miracle of Christmas was my shift of attitude. Our Christmas traditions had gotten in the way of the true meaning of the season. I had been so focused on doing what we'd done before, I forgot the reason we have Christmas.

I also realized that the mystery and warmth of Christmas can be felt even in an impersonal hospital room. Since then, each year, our family goes to the hospital on Christmas Eve and we visit the children. We sing Christmas carols and bring gift baskets to brighten their Christmas just as ours was brightened when Katie spent Christmas in the hospital.

That Christmas had been a miracle for us; we wanted to help make miracles for other children.

24. The Christmas Guest

Donna Dawson

THE WIND HOWLED THROUGH THE EAVES OF OUR CENTURY-old house. I was eight years old and young enough to romp in the backyard in spite of the growing storm. The rest of the family was inside preparing our Christmas dinner.

I finally left my outside play and went back into the house. As I opened the door, the aroma of turkey and baking pies filled the house. Before long, Mom called us to the table and we were ready for our Christmas feast.

Just then, the doorbell rang. Rising from her place opposite my father, Mom made her way to the hall and the front door.

An old woman stood there. She held a covered birdcage. "Could I have some lettuce for my bunny? And my coat's torn. Would you have some thread and a needle?"

By then I had gotten up and stood behind my mother and stared. The gray-haired woman looked old. She was wrapped in an odd assortment of rags. Gray hair stuck out of a worn hat. Her curls seemed like a mixture of grease and dampness. Her cheeks were sunken and lined. Most of all, she stank and I guessed it was because she hadn't had a bath in a long time.

I wanted Mom to close the door so we could eat. Instead,

Mom stepped aside and with a sweep of her work-worn hand, welcomed the old woman into the dining room. She told her to sit in a chair opposite me. Her body odor didn't make me want to smile.

My curiosity, however, soon overcame my revulsion as I stared at the scrawny bunny curled up in a corner of the birdcage. She held the cage on her lap with a tight grip, as if she were afraid to lose her only companion.

Dad rose and silently went into the kitchen. He returned shortly afterward with a large lettuce leaf and a jar lid filled with water. The rabbit attacked the lettuce as though it hadn't eaten in weeks.

With a look of relief, the woman lowered the cage to the floor by her feet. I couldn't see the rabbit but I could hear it chewing.

The woman ate with us. Mom waited on her as though she were a queen. She even gave her the choice parts of the turkey and heaped dressing, potatoes, gravy, and vegetables on her plate. For dessert, Mom gave her the biggest slice of pie.

There wasn't much conversation. "Where are you going?" Dad asked.

She named a city about ten miles away.

She didn't volunteer any more information so Dad didn't say anything more to her.

Like the rabbit, the woman hungrily ate everything. She didn't say another word—she was too busy shoveling in the food. Finally, she leaned back and smiled. She wiped at her mouth with dainty gestures that surprised me. For the first time I looked into her eyes. Although I was only eight, I sensed that deep within her blue eyes was an aching sadness and shame.

She smiled and thanked my mother.

After the meal, Mom said, "You sit right down." She indicated her own favorite chair. "I'll get the thread." Mom stitched the gaping tear in the woman's coat. While our guest settled near the fire and seemed to draw from its heat, we six children cleared the table and washed the dishes.

We hurried through our chores because we wanted to stare at the old woman. She put the rabbit in its cage next to her feet. The lettuce was gone and he had finished most of the water.

Dad came into the living room and handed her a small bag. "Food," he said. "Something for you to eat along the way."

She smiled and thanked him.

"I put in extra lettuce for the rabbit."

After Mom had mended the coat, our guest pulled herself to her feet and put on the well-worn coat.

"Won't you stay?" Dad asked. "The snow is heavy out there right now. It might be that way for another hour or so."

She shook her head.

"I would be pleased to drive you to where you want to go."

She shook her head, thanked my parents, and bundled the birdcage up tight in a large scrap of toweling.

We crowded around and watched her slip into her several layers of clothes. I wondered what would cause a person like her—especially an old woman—to wander in such a violent storm. She slipped her feet into a pair of old rubber boots. She looked up and smiled at us. "Thank you," she said.

Dad again tried to get her to stay, but she refused.

To many people this may not sound like a miracle, but it was to me. No Christmas before or since has affected me like that one. I had been only a child. To me, Christmas meant celebrating and receiving presents.

My parents enabled me to understand the miracle of Christmas. This was like the holy family in the Bible: They came to a strange town and had to sleep in a place alongside the animals. The old woman had come to us, a stranger, scraggly and dirty, but my parents opened their hearts to her as if she had been an old friend. Their kindness to the old woman gave me an example of true Christianity—they gave themselves to her and expected nothing in return. They demonstrated love in action.

It was the best sermon I ever heard in my life.

25. The Birthday Party

Shari McMinn

FOR CHRISTMAS OF 1995, OUR FAMILY SHARED MY PARENTS'
mountain home with my siblings and our assorted kids, who
numbered more than a dozen. My parents were delighted for us
to be together.

Dad, whom we affectionately called Poppy, had grown up during the Great Depression with his brother and widowed mother.
Their home never saw abundance. Now, close to retirement, he
was pleased to be able to share generously with his children and
grandchildren the type of Christmas he never had.

After the flurry of morning gift unwrapping, the eating
frenzy began with brunch and continued until the evening buf-
fet. During the late-morning food preparation, my ten-month-
old daughter, Abby, ran a low-grade fever and spit up frequently.
Assuming it was teething and a mild cold, our festivities continued while her aunts, grandmother, and I traded her off from
one set of arms to another.

She didn't get any better. My younger sister suggested we
call her pediatrician. He prescribed medication and said, "If she
isn't markedly better within six hours, take her to the local
emergency room."

We gave Abby the first dose around three o'clock. We assumed all was well, and continued to enjoy our day. By late afternoon Abby was fussy enough that I passed on the horse-drawn sleigh ride Poppy had arranged for everyone. Instead, Abby and I sat on the sofa, in front of a roaring fire, watching a holiday movie.

After the sleigh riders returned, the house filled with noise and activity until it was time to start the multitude of baths for the younger children. Abby was the last to be ready for bed. As my husband, Cary, was toweling her off, my sister remarked that she looked pale. The six hours had passed and she hadn't gotten better.

After Cary and I decided to take her to the ER, Poppy volunteered to drive us. The roads were icy, but he knew the roads well. Because I had bundled Abby in a bulky snowsuit and she whimpered, I wanted to hold her. That wasn't usual because Cary and I had always buckled up our kids. Despite her fever, Abby was awake, and smiled sweetly. I rocked her gently and she fell asleep less than a mile from the house.

About ten minutes into the twenty-five-minute ride to the hospital, Abby stopped breathing. I yelled to Cary and Poppy, "Stop!" Then I cried out, "No! Keep going! Call 911!" Finally I screamed, "Drive to the fire station just around the corner. They can give her CPR!"

As Poppy raced into the fire station driveway, he laid his hand on the horn. As soon as he braked, Cary grabbed Abby and rushed to the door. He rang the bell. Rousted out of their sleep on a quiet night, the rescue workers immediately began CPR and called for an ambulance. They continued giving CPR until the ambulance arrived.

They loaded our precious baby into the back of the vehicle. Cary jumped in with her. Poppy pushed his car at top speed and we stayed right behind them. During the trip that seemed interminable, I prayed and cried while grieving Poppy tried to comfort me as he drove through the ice and snow.

Hours later in the ER waiting room, we received the news that Abby never regained consciousness. (Her autopsy showed that she had been a healthy, well-cared-for baby who had contracted a one-in-a-million virus. It traveled through her bloodstream to her heart.)

It was such a heartbreaking tragedy for us. And the fact that it happened on Christmas made it seem worse. *This is Christmas. This is the day that's supposed to be filled with joy and happiness.*

We returned home with empty arms. Neither of us slept much that night and we wondered how we would tell Abby's five siblings what had happened. Because we left with her after they were in bed, none of them knew we had taken their sister to the hospital.

"How can they understand?" I asked Cary. I asked God, "How can we comfort them when we're in such grief?" No matter how hard I prayed, I couldn't think of anything to say to comfort them.

As soon as the kids were up the next morning, between his own sobs, Cary explained that Abby had gone to heaven to be with Jesus.

My then four-year-old son said, "That's wonderful! She got to go to Jesus' birthday party!"

Those words didn't take away our pain, but they brought peace to us. That simple response made us realize that our son had grasped the truth we hadn't been able to accept. It wasn't just that Abby was dead. He understood: She had gone to the great celebration with Jesus.

26. "Let's Play, Mommy!"

Lisa-Anne Wooldridge

"I'M SORRY. WE'RE DOING EVERYTHING WE CAN."

The doctors did everything they could to save my son's life.

I called Jesse my miracle baby. Born three months prematurely, he'd amazed everyone with his fighting spirit and will to live. He'd kept his sweet nature through many traumas and life-threatening illnesses over the next seven years.

This time, however, nothing seemed to work. Jesse looked so small and helpless with wires and tubes attached everywhere. I wanted to pray for him, to simply ask God to heal him, but I was too tired. We'd repeated this scene so many times that I'd developed prayer fatigue.

Now, three days before Christmas, I could see the fight going out of him. I could feel it draining out of me, too. Trying to place Jesse in God's hands, I looked up at the silent television. *Please, God*, I thought, *don't let us have a Christmas tragedy. On TV, they always have Christmas miracles. I know you can write a better story than that.*

As Jesse struggled to breathe, his abdomen retracted deeply in the attempt. He had a dangerous kind of croup and his airway was extremely narrow from the inflamed scar tissue that lined his throat. Lucille Packard Children's Hospital at Stanford, in northern California, was one of the best in the nation. The staff was doing all they could.

It just wasn't enough.

I leaned my head against the cool glass of the hospital window, breathing slowly and deeply. *Oh, dear, loving God,* I cried silently, *I wish I could breathe for him.* And Jesse wasn't the only sick child there. In the rooms around us lay other desperately ill children with equally worried parents. The atmosphere felt heavy with sadness. For me, it seemed to match the grayness of the day outside.

A whimper and a look of pain on Jesse's face made me realize he was worse than he had been.

Christmas should be about good news. Why should there be such sadness at this time of year? As I pondered what to do, I decided to call others and ask for their prayers.

"I'm going to call people to pray for you." I pushed back the tears as I said to my son, "You're going to be okay."

I made the calls and waited. I pulled him close to me and held him as tightly as I dared. As I stared out the window, darkness slowly descended. I was afraid of the darkness, because Jesse always went downhill in the evenings. The doctors had already told me that we should expect an especially rough night.

Just then someone knocked at the door. I called out, "Come in."

Two huge men entered the room. Between their size and their smiles, they seemed to fill the room. They were members of the San Jose Sharks, a professional hockey team. "We've come to bring a little Christmas cheer to the children," one of them said.

Jesse loved visitors, no matter how ill he was, and he waved them to come closer. Holding his toys, he strained to whisper, "I have two cars." He held up one of the shiny Matchbox toys. "Can you find a boy in another room who doesn't have any and give him this one? Tell him I'll be his friend."

As the hockey players left, both of them had tears in their eyes.

"Thank you for this wonderful little boy," I prayed. "The world needs boys like him!"

As the staff had predicted, it was a hard night, and not just for us. Alarms buzzed all over that wing of the hospital. I stood guard as Jesse held on, needing many treatments with powerful drugs just to keep breathing. I repeatedly reminded myself of a verse from the book of Psalms, "Weeping may last through the night but joy comes with the morning" (Psalm 30:5). I didn't know if God would make it come true for me, but I determined to recite the verse and hold on.

With the sunrise came more dark clouds and rain. The doctors didn't communicate with us and the nurses looked sad when they walked into the room. Jesse couldn't stay awake for more than a few minutes at a time. My apprehension grew.

As discouragement pulled at me, I thought of a church where I'd visited a few times. The people there had seemed genuine and I felt such a spirit of love whenever I visited. As the morning wore on, I couldn't stop thinking about them. "They care

about people. They pray for people," I said to myself. As difficult as it was to share the pain of what we were going through,
I called my friend Jessica. "Please contact the minister and the
people at that church. Ask them—ask them if they'll pray for
Jesse, will you?"

Jessica was delighted to be able to do something for us.

For a long time I stared at my little boy. The dark circles under his eyes had deepened. They came from the effort it took to
draw each breath. I wanted to wipe away the bruises on the
bridge of his nose that came from wearing the oxygen mask. His
curly hair was damp and tangled, but he looked like an angel to
me, as beautiful as any I'd seen in paintings or on Christmas
cards.

I got up and walked to the window and stared into space.
Just then, a bright rainbow filled the sky right in front of me. I
didn't understand it, but I felt God had sent that rainbow just
for me. I kept repeating, "Thank you! Thank you, Lord!" As I
watched, three layers of cloud cover parted just above our window and revealed the blue sky.

"It's like an open heaven," I whispered. I can't explain it, but
I believed that not only was the rainbow just for me, but I also
felt God had given me a special sign. "I'll take that as a promise, God. I trust you to take care of him!" As deep peace washed
over me, I was ready to curl up next to Jesse and rest.

I didn't know it then, but word had spread quickly throughout the community about our son. People made phone calls and
sent e-mails all over the country asking for prayer.

Just then, I realized Jesse wasn't wheezing. He looked so

peaceful, my first thought was that he had died. But the alarms were silent. No, I assured myself, he's breathing deeply and easily on his own.

Within minutes, my son, who had struggled for every breath during the night and lay listless and unmoving, grinned at me. He sat up in bed. He yanked off his mask and disconnected the wire. "Let's play, Mommy!"

Immediately the alarms sounded because of his actions. Nurses rushed in, expecting a crisis. Instead there were shocked expressions and disbelief on their faces.

Jesse jumped out of bed and ran around the room. Afraid he might relapse, I scooped him up and hugged him. The tears came freely now and I knew God had answered prayer—my prayer and those of hundreds of others.

One of the nurses asked, "What happened in here?"

"God's helping me," Jesse replied matter-of-factly. "He's helping all the children." The nurses called the doctors with the good news. Within an hour of reaching out for prayer, everything had changed.

We had to stay another day for observation, so we sent out e-mails of thanks. Jesse and I enjoyed the day playing together, and we watched holiday movies. We prayed for the other families on our floor, too.

Very early Christmas Eve morning, Jesse woke up and said, "Mommy, Jesus came to see me. He said I'm going to be all better. It was special. He's telling the other kids stories in their rooms right now." He smiled, lay back, closed his eyes, and was soon asleep.

I lay awake with tears of joy sliding down my face. "Thank you," I prayed, "he's coming home for Christmas."

That night was the most peaceful night we'd ever experienced in the pediatric ICU. Nurses remarked on how quiet it was, how strange that no alarms broke the silence. There were no crying children and no sudden crises. It was as if a sweet peace had fallen over the entire hospital wing and everyone was able to rest.

"You gave us a good ending to our story, Lord," I said. "It's even better than TV."

God had helped my son to breathe when the doctors couldn't. After years of fighting for his life and spending far too much time in intensive care, it turned out just as Jesse said: Jesus had made him well. Even better, our son hasn't been hospitalized since. Even the scars are gone.

Since then, whenever troubles come, I no longer hesitate to call people for prayer. Jesse won't let me. He still believes in miracles.

So do I.

27. The Magical Twenty

Virginia B. Tenery

DURING THE CHRISTMAS SEASON OF 1981, I LIVED COMfortably under somewhat spartan circumstances in a small town outside Dallas, Texas. I had a good job in the city and made enough to support the three of us; however, it meant an eighty-mile trip to work and back—a small price to pay for job security in that troubled economic period. Another plus for me was that the benefits of country living more than compensated for the long commute into the sprawling city.

One of the big rewards was the rural church we attended. We felt we belonged and that the people there loved us. My mother, daughter, and I rarely missed a service. None of the members were wealthy, but they had earned a well-deserved reputation for helping the less fortunate in our neighborhood.

The Sunday before Christmas we went to church and were delighted to see that the building was full. Most people had forgone Christmas travel because of the economic situation.

Just before the pastor dismissed us, he made an unusual request. "I want to take up a love offering for a former pastor of this church. He mentored me when I first entered the ministry. Today I received heartbreaking news. He has cancer." Our pastor brushed away his tears and explained that the man was too ill to serve his congregation. His church hadn't provided health insurance, and he also said that the congregation couldn't help him now, although he didn't know the reason.

"He and his wife are trying to survive on his Social Security payments. They need our help, especially now at Christmas." He paused and stared at us before he added, "I think we need to pray about adding him to our missionary support fund."

One of our deacons stood up. "I don't think we need to pray about adding him to the missionary list. I make a motion that we do it."

Another man seconded the motion and it passed without dissent.

That need touched my heart. I wanted to contribute, but I had a problem. Because of Christmas expenses, I had no money except for a twenty-dollar bill inside my purse. I needed that to buy gas the following week.

What should I do? God, should I give my last twenty dollars? I didn't hear any voice, but I sensed I knew the answer. When the offering plate reached me, I dropped in my twenty-dollar bill.

Most of us stayed at church until the deacons counted the offering. "We collected eight hundred dollars," the pastor announced. "I'll take it to the family tonight."

I smiled and felt I had done the right thing. I had no idea how I'd buy gas, but the old pastor's needs far surpassed my own. I drove home in a warm glow, and felt good about my decision.

It wasn't until Wednesday that I began to worry. During the

long trek home from work, the needle on my gas gauge inched its way toward empty. I'd made the trip so many times I could tell from the gauge that I had enough fuel to get me home, but not enough to get to work the next day.

Over dinner that night my concerns must have reflected on my face.

"Something wrong at work, honey?" my mother asked.

I shook my head. "Everything's fine at work." That wasn't a lie and I didn't want her to worry.

Calling in sick was an option, but lying to my boss wasn't. Also, I needed to be at work Thursday to pick up my paycheck before the three-day Christmas weekend began.

After dinner I again pushed aside my problem and spent time with Holly, my daughter. Her excitement bubbled over with Christmas near and holiday activities at church. As a working mom I had little time to spend with her, so I gave her my full attention until bedtime.

Thursday morning was Christmas Eve day. I dressed for work. *God, I've done what I thought was right. I'm glad I was able to help that needy couple. Now I have a money problem. I need to get to work. Please get me to work without running out of gas.*

Just before breakfast, I reminded myself that Jesus had once fed five thousand with five small loaves and two fish.

Over a breakfast of toast and coffee, Mom turned to me. "Don't forget to leave Holly's ticket for the church hayride." Her Sunday school teacher would pick her up after lunch.

I had bought the ticket a week earlier. I reached into my billfold for the ticket. Inside was a twenty-dollar bill. I gasped. "Did you put money in my purse?"

"No, I might have if I had any money," Mom said. "Why?"

I held up the bill. "I don't know where it came from." I told her about giving my last twenty dollars in the offering.

We smiled, laughed, praised, and thanked God before I left.

We never did find out where the money had come from. I didn't need a logical explanation. I had given every cent I had to someone in need. God had heard my prayer and also provided for me in my need.

Although I had been taught that God provides for our needs, this was a big test for me. God did provide.

I felt a deep sense of joy and inner peace. I had been an answer to someone's prayer; some unknown person had been an answer to mine. *That's how God works,* I thought. *When we do what we can, God does what he can.*

We had a wonderful Christmas because I reached out to a needy family. And because I reached out to them, God reached out to me.

28. The Question

Donna Teti

MY TWIN SISTER, SUE, AND I LIVED IN THE SAME TOWN. While the kids were in school, we happily had long conversations each morning as we prepared for Christmas.

Those exciting Christmas calls continued for years, and we shared gift ideas for our kids, our husbands, and our parents. We often shopped together and planned family activities. We mentioned sales, shared recipes, talked about parties, and went over details of the traditional Christmas dinner our two families shared together each Christmas Day.

Sue died suddenly of a stroke in the spring. I grieved for months and couldn't seem to get past my sense of loss. I missed her most during the Christmas season. There would be no morning chats, no coffee, and no shopping together. *How could I enjoy Christmas without my sister? Please, dear God, help me get through this Christmas and find joy along the way.*

When I saw a sign in the window of the local craft store for a seasonal floral designer, impulsively I went inside and applied for the job. Days later, I wondered if I had made the right decision. I thought that by taking the job during the Christmas season I would fill the lonely hours during the day when I missed my sister the most. By interacting with others, I could push away my grief.

But the floral-designer booth was tucked away in the far corner of the store. I couldn't talk to any customers unless they came back to where I worked, asking where to find an item in the store. Worse, I worked alone. It will only be for a few weeks, I told myself, and it's better to keep busy. Several times, I prayed, "God, please let me find some joy in this job."

Each day, I routinely walked around the store and collected ornaments, Christmas flowers, or Christmas balls to create beautiful wreaths or to put into baskets. To my surprise, I became so involved in my work that I didn't mind being alone.

Some days I made the traditional baskets or wreaths filled with red poinsettias, holly, and evergreens. Other times I placed a teddy bear in the middle with cute, red bows around it and added small bells. Sometimes I created a more elaborate piece with pink or plum Christmas flowers adorned with a gold or silver angel.

I left each afternoon with ten to fifteen pieces finished and displayed in the front of the store. The next morning when I came in, most of them had been sold.

A week before Christmas, I was focused on keeping up with creating last-minute pieces.

"Are you having fun?"

Startled, I jumped and then I laughed.

An elderly man stood in front of me. He wore a yellow and black plaid winter coat. He had wavy white hair and a kind smile.

"Actually, I am." The words popped out of my mouth.

I stared at him, waiting for him to ask about where to buy something. Instead he stood there and smiled.

Embarrassed at staring, I dropped my head and looked at the arrangement I had been working on before he came. He said nothing more.

I looked up again to ask if he needed any help.

He was gone.

I looked around the area, but I didn't see him. I wondered where he had gone so quickly. "Funny question," I said to myself. And just then, I realized that I had answered him correctly: I was having fun.

A few days before Christmas Eve, again I worked intently at one of my latest creations, a wreath with a peace dove, white poinsettias, and blue and silver ribbons. It would be one of my final wreaths before Christmas. I attached the blue and silver bow to the bottom of the wreath.

"Are you having fun?"

Startled, I looked up. An elderly woman wrapped in a blue wool coat smiled at me.

How strange, I thought, *to have a second person ask the same question.* "Yes, yes, I am having fun. Thank you."

Like the elderly man of the week before, she asked nothing but just stood there. Like him, she smiled warmly and I thought she looked absolutely contented. Feeling slightly embarrassed, I looked away just as I had before. When I looked up, only seconds later, she was gone.

This time, I left my booth and searched for the elderly

woman in the blue wool coat. I went up and down the aisles. I knew I wouldn't find her. I can't explain how I knew, but I did. I also felt a deep peace.

I stopped and smiled. I'd heard of angels grabbing people out of the flames of a burning house, from a car crash, or from drowning. Maybe God sent two angels to me to help me realize I *was* having fun and that I was going to be okay. The pain of losing my twin had begun to diminish.

I fully believe they were both angels—sent by a loving God to bring to my attention that he heard me and answered my prayer. I did find joy that Christmas season, even while I grieved.

The healing had begun.

29. "Thank You, Amen"

Elizabeth M. Harbuck with Marley Gibson

"EXPLOITIVE DERMATITIS," THE DOCTOR SAID. THAT WAS the best diagnosis my husband, Joe, received for his unexplained skin disease.

One night he went to bed and felt quite normal; the next morning he awoke with something broken out all over his body. It looked like a mix between measles, chicken pox, and psoriasis. The strange eruption covered every part of his body from the top of his head to the bottom of his feet. As bad as that was, he itched constantly. He scratched himself so much that he had to wear gloves because the ends of his fingers had split open.

We took Joe to the clinic every week, hoping and praying each time that they could explain his skin disease. They tried every available medication on him. Nothing worked.

All through his ordeal, Joe never missed a day of work, and he didn't complain. "It came quickly overnight and it will go away just as quickly," he said several times.

I hoped he was right. I called it Job's disease. In the Bible it says that Job was struck "with terrible boils from head to foot" (Job 2:7).

We learned about two other men in our area with a similar disease. We wished we hadn't. One committed suicide and they admitted the other to what they called an asylum in those days.

On September 23, 1970, my parents visited to welcome home my medical doctor brother, David, and his wife. David had completed his tour of army duty in Germany.

After an enjoyable evening together Joe stood up. "I'm not feeling well." He excused himself and went down the hallway to our bedroom.

"Liz! Liz!" he screamed not long after that.

I ran toward him. "I'm coming—"

"Get David and come quickly!"

David and I rushed to the master bedroom. David examined Joe quietly and efficiently. "I'm sorry to tell you, but you're having a heart attack."

We arranged for relatives to stay with our three children and rushed Joe to the hospital. At the emergency room, David identified himself as a medical doctor. "My brother-in-law has had a myocardial infarction."

The nurses hurried into action and sent for the cardiologist. They put Joe on a gurney and moved him into the intensive care unit. In 1970, in New England where we lived, they didn't know as much about heart attack patients as they do today. Back then, they normally gave them injections of morphine and watched them closely.

Joe spent several days in the hospital. He was weak. It exhausted him just to have one of us wheel him down the hallway for a shower by the orderly.

Feelings of sadness and fear swept over me. As much as I tried not to, I wondered what I would do without Joe. He was only forty-three years old. As much as I could, I tried to focus on gratitude to God that he was still alive.

There was one bright spot in that terrible ordeal. As Joe had predicted, his skin condition cleared up. Doctors later said the stress had built up inside his body and caused the skin condition. His heart attack was the "breaking point" and released everything inside of him.

After about a week, Joe came home. He slowly began to recuperate. Three months later, on December 9, 1970, Joe suffered another massive coronary—on the fifteenth birthday of our daughter, Jennifer. After an examination at the hospital, the doctor came out to the waiting room. The gravity of his face warned me of the message.

"I'm sorry, but your husband is gravely ill—"

"How ill?"

"He won't make it through the night." As my tears erupted he said softly, "Go home and prepare your children."

I left the hospital. I wasn't emotionally ready to face our three children. I wanted to wait until my two older children, Jeff and Jennifer, were out of school. I'm not sure why, but I stopped and bought an artificial Christmas tree, the kind that comes inside a box.

I picked up Jeff and Jennifer and drove them home, and Jeff immediately assembled the tree and Jennifer started to decorate. While I waited for four-year-old Marley to come home from the neighbors, I went into the bedroom and called a few friends at church. I told them about Joe and asked them to pray.

When I heard Marley's voice, I returned to the children. I took a deep breath and prayed silently for guidance before I said, "Kids, sit down. Your dad's back in the hospital."

Marley, hands on her hips, stared defiantly at me, and asked, "What's wrong with my daddy?"

I knelt in front of her so that we were on the same eye level. "The doctors say that Daddy might go home to be with Jesus tonight." I bit my lip so that I wouldn't cry. I had tried to pray, but I didn't know how. I didn't even know if I should pray for Joe's recovery. That wasn't the kind of praying we did in our church. We prayed for God's will to be done. Of course I wanted him well, but was it right to ask God to intervene?

Just then, Marley clasped her hands together and looked toward the ceiling. "Dear God, please make my daddy well. Thank you, amen." She turned around and picked up one of her toys.

Even in my pain, I smiled. I had struggled with how to pray. Our little daughter certainly taught me about prayer that night. She went directly to her source: She made her petition to God; she thanked him before he answered; and she rested positively after her request.

Moved by her simple expression of faith, I relaxed. I couldn't explain it, but Marley's simple prayer changed my attitude. I *knew* God had heard her. I sat down at the piano and started to play and sing hymns. Between them, I paused to say, "Thank you, God."

Word about Joe spread rapidly through our church group, and

several people came to the house to stand vigil with me that night. Their kindness touched me and I told them so. I went back to the piano to play and sing praises to God.

"She's still in shock," I overheard one friend say. Another thought I was in denial about Joe's impending death. It was neither. I told them that God had heard my daughter's prayer.

Joe didn't die that night. The next morning, he was extremely weak, but still alive.

The children and I were allowed to spend Christmas Day with him in his hospital room. We brought a miniature Christmas tree and gifts for him. We were grateful to have Christmas time together.

I had great peace. It came from such a simple thing as a prayer from a child who didn't know enough about his medical condition to understand that her daddy was supposed to die. Marley had enough faith to believe in a God who cared enough to listen to her prayer. A simple prayer, and just as sweetly and simply, she had said, "Thank you, amen."

Joe lived and is still alive today, four decades later. I don't understand what happened and I don't try to explain it. This much I know: A child prayed with utter faith that God would hear her and let her father live and God answered.

30. A Christmas Lesson

Suzan L. Wiener

CHRISTMAS HAD ALWAYS BEEN A SPECIAL TIME FOR ME. Until *that* year. In the past, we had filled our house with the holiday spirit and love of family and friends. This year my house wasn't gaily decorated with candy canes, snowflakes, and silver tinsel, and that saddened me.

Why, God, did you let this happen? I'm only forty and now my life is over. Why, God?

God didn't answer.

No one visited me; no one called. I stopped praying. Why should I pray? Everyone had ignored me. Even God had abandoned me. My back hurt all the time and I didn't know the cause.

Being in a hospital on Christmas was lonely enough, but when the Christmas cards and decorative wreaths began to appear, I felt even more alone. Why didn't my friends visit? Where was my family when I needed them? They had their own families. But I was family, too. I had assumed they would visit. Where was God when I hurt and felt abandoned by everyone?

My heart was breaking. I hurt too deeply for tears to reach the surface.

The nurses could see how sad I was and they tried to be friendly. They assured me, "Oh, you'll get better" and "You'll go home soon." Several of them came into my room to share Christmas candy they had received from former patients.

I missed my husband and I understood why he wasn't there. I understood but that didn't stop the loneliness. Howard was with his terminally ill mother. He had his own anguish between wanting to be with me and being by her bedside during her last days.

"It's all right," I assured him. "You need to be there. I'll be all right."

But I wasn't all right. He called me several times a day—and that helped a little. As soon as we hung up, I stared at the antiseptic walls and my loneliness took over the room.

I was in physical pain—that was bad enough—but I was also frightened. Perhaps the fear made my loneliness more serious. For the acute back pain they gave me frequent muscle relaxants, which lulled me into a sedated sleep. I didn't know what was going to happen to me and no one told me.

The doctor finally came in. He read my chart, looked at me, and said matter-of-factly, "Your MRI came in."

I looked up expecting good news.

"You have herniated disk disease."

"What does that mean?"

"If your back goes out again, it could leave you paralyzed." He turned around and walked out.

I stared at the closed door. *Great bedside manner, Doctor.*

Self-pity overwhelmed me. I yearned to be in my own home,

in my comfortable bed, not lying in such a cold, sterile environment. The nurses were friendly enough, but they wanted to be home with their families. I couldn't blame them for that.

I had no one to talk to, no one to hold my hand or encourage me. Between the inner conflict and physical pain, I suffered in silence. *Why? Why is this happening to me? What did I do to deserve this?*

God still didn't answer.

The next morning the staff brought in a roommate named Marcy. She was a frail, older woman, who seemed to be in physical agony. I couldn't feel any compassion for her: I was too occupied with my own pain.

She slept most of the time, although sometimes I heard her praying. One time she cried aloud, "Please, dear God, help my friend in the next bed. Give her comfort and peace."

I thought God didn't hear her. Why should he hear her anyway? He hasn't listened to me.

A new thought struck me. She had prayed for me. Why would she pray for me? She doesn't know me. We'll be together in this room a few days and never see each other again. I don't even want to talk to her.

But she wanted to talk to me. Whenever Marcy was awake, she'd call over, "How are you feeling? How's the pain?" Simple, caring questions and gentle nudges, and they finally broke through my resistance.

I slowly opened up to her. She told me about her family—and her words made it clear how much she loved them. She didn't talk much about herself, but mostly about the family.

Marcy had suffered for years from heart problems and diabetes. Now she had cancer. Despite all her physical problems, her faith remained vibrant. She talked about God giving her the strength and courage to face her illnesses.

I wouldn't admit it, but I was envious of her sustained faith in God.

Christmas morning her family came to visit. It was a large family: three daughters and their husbands, and quite a number of grandchildren. Her family's expressions of affection seemed to strengthen her body as well as her faith.

Marcy introduced me to the family. To my surprise, they included me in their joyful expression and conversations. "Anything I can do for you, Suzan?" I heard that question several times. And I felt they meant it.

Marcy seemed to forget her own pain while they were in the room. They laughed and talked and the warmth of their words touched me. A granddaughter, Cindy, gave me a beautifully embroidered handkerchief.

The tears I hadn't been able to shed before gushed out of me.

After they left, Marcy asked, "Could we pray together?"

"All right," I said, "go ahead." I meant she would pray and I would listen. That went on two or three nights. Finally, I was able to pray for her and for myself. As I did, a warm, uplifting feeling came over me. My back still hurt as much as ever, but my spirit had been healed. Hope began to grow inside my heart. Eventually I had surgery and experienced relief from my physical pain.

But I had an even more important healing. The week after

Christmas I went home. But by then I was different. I believed in God once again. I felt as if I were a new person. Most of the time I was happy, even joyous.

That Christmas in the hospital I learned one of the best lessons of my life—and it was also one of my favorite Christmases. Marcy's family pulled me into their hearts, asking nothing in return. They loved me when I couldn't love myself.

Marcy left the hospital a few days before I did. But that wasn't the end. She came back every day to visit me. "Do you need anything?" she asked each time. And I sensed she meant it.

Marcy and I continued to stay in contact. She always asked, "Do you need anything?" We prayed for each other. I felt God had answered my prayers for her because she looked better and said she felt better.

God did answer. But I had been slow to hear.

God had granted me a Christmas miracle, one that will always be with me. Even now, years later, when I start to falter or question God's love or presence, I think of my wonderful friend, Marcy. She made me understand God's love. She became God's human hands that touched a lonely, self-pitying woman, and made her know that God hadn't forgotten her.

31. Poinsettias from God

Emila Belk

"LORD, I'D REALLY LIKE TO HAVE A POINSETTIA FOR CHRIST-mas. I know I don't *need* one, but it sure would make me happy." I prayed that prayer without telling anyone, knowing that the only way I'd get a poinsettia was through God's provision. *If God wants me to have a poinsettia, he'll give me one.*

Maybe that sounds like a petty prayer, but I love poinsettias at Christmastime. Something about the bright red flowers gives me joy, and I needed joy that year. My husband and I were in the midst of heavy financial troubles and didn't feel we could afford anything extra. He was without a full-time job and had experienced several health problems. Most of the family burdens became my responsibility. I wondered how we'd provide for the essentials, let alone Christmas presents for the children.

I decorated the house as best I could for the holidays, but my heart wasn't in it. I didn't want to decorate; I did it for the kids. I was sad because I wanted things I knew I couldn't have. Seeing festive decorations in stores and in other people's homes, and hearing the fun things others were doing only made me sadder.

The Sunday before Christmas our family went to church.

My husband taught the high school Sunday school class and I taught the women's class. Between Sunday school and the worship service, I went into the narthex to visit friends. I watched my husband climb the stairs. His arms held an awkward pile of things. He had gifts from his students: packages of candy, books, and cards. I spotted a small, green pot with a beautiful red flower peeking out.

"Where did you get that?"

"Lauren gave it to me," Steve said. "It was nice of her, but it's kind of a strange gift for a man."

"Oh, no. That's *my* poinsettia. Don't even think that it's for you." He stared at me and I said, "This is a gift straight from the hands of God for *me*. I prayed for a poinsettia, and God answered!"

God showed me that year that he cares about poinsettias and he cares even more for me.

By the following Christmas our finances hadn't improved. However, rather than pray for a live poinsettia again, I decided to get by with the fake poinsettia stems stored in my box of Christmas decorations. They were left from the days we owned a bookstore. As fake as they were, they would add splashes of color throughout the house and give it a more festive feel.

I worked the imitation red flowers in with the decorations on the fireplace mantel. I stuck them in baskets. I inserted them between the branches of the Christmas tree. I laid them on shelves. They didn't look special, just okay, but I was determined to be content. Each time I looked at one of the poinsettia stems, I remembered God's goodness to me the year before.

On the last day of school before Christmas break, our friends Rick and Nancy visited us. Rick is the head custodian at the nearby elementary school. They came into the house carrying two huge poinsettia plants, one red and one white.

"We thought you might enjoy these. We know how much you love poinsettias." Nancy placed the two foiled pots on my kitchen counter. "They were left over from the kids' Christmas program."

I stared at how big and beautiful they were. Bright red flowers. Big white flowers. "I've never had a white poinsettia." Tears glided down my cheeks as I said those words.

I accepted that gift as if God had personally delivered them. There wasn't a handwritten note that came with the poinsettias, but I understood the divine message: *I love you. I haven't forgotten you.*

"You'll never know how much these poinsettias mean to me." New tears formed in my eyes as I thanked Rick and Nancy several more times. I explained that I had prayed for a poinsettia the year before and God had provided, but "This year I decided to get by without a real one. I guess God knows the desires of my heart."

My friends were delighted to be part of that special blessing from God.

The next year at Christmastime, our friend Jim called. "Janet and I have something for you. Is it okay if I come over and drop it off?" When Jim rang the doorbell, he held a poinsettia in his hands. "We remembered how much you love poinsettias. We saw this and thought of you."

Again I cried at God's goodness.

We've had many lean years, but God has blessed each Christmas with a gift of a poinsettia. They're not always from the same people; they are always from the same God. No matter how they come to me, I see them as miracles.

Poinsettias have become symbolic to me. They represent God's goodness. Each year at Christmas, they remind me that nothing is too small for God's attention. If it's important to me, it's important to him.

32. A Lucky Christmas Miracle

Dave Schrader

SADNESS HAD FILLED OUR HOUSE FOR WEEKS—EVER SINCE the death of our family dog, Cagney. Our young son, Nathan, missed Cagney and so did we. The loss was so hard on us that we agreed to buy a new puppy, a basset hound, for Christmas.

When I brought the puppy home, I had Nathan with me as well as a friend and his son. As soon as I got to the door, I realized I had forgotten to pick up the house key when we left. The door had locked behind me.

I didn't know what to do. It would be several hours before my wife returned from work. The weather was near freezing and the two young boys had become restless. I tried each door of the house and every window, but nothing budged. "The only thing left to do," I said to myself, "is to break a window in the garage."

The others got back inside my car and I went around to the back of the garage. I tried to push open the back window, but it was locked from the inside. Reluctantly, I reached down and grabbed a stone from the garden, and struck the window as hard as I could. Nothing happened, so I repeated the action twice. The window refused to break.

Exasperated I looked to the sky and called out, "Okay, God, if you have a better plan, I am listening."

I set the stone down and pushed on the window. To my amazement, it swung open. "How did that happen?" I asked.

I crawled inside and raced through the house to the front door to let the others in. Once we were inside, I returned to the garage to check the window damage. I was sure the latch had torn free from the sill. I reached the window and tried to open it. Again it wouldn't budge. I went outside and pushed. The window stubbornly refused to yield. I returned to the warmth of the garage and inspected the window, still unable to understand how it had swung open for me only minutes earlier only to be shut and locked now with no damage to the glass, latch, or framing. I shrugged, smiled, and thanked God before I joined the others in the living room.

Within minutes, the puppy sniffed about as if looking for a place to go to the toilet. I carried him to the back door and let him out on the deck. Right then, my son needed his diaper changed. Just about the time I finished changing the diaper, I heard loud yelps from the deck. They were yelps of pain.

I left Nathan with my friend and ran to the deck. The puppy had fallen off our second-story deck and had landed on the concrete ground below. He lay there barking in pain, but he wasn't moving.

I hurried down and lifted the puppy into my arms. Sad wails came from him whenever I moved his body. His poor little body was curved backward like a crescent moon. I wrapped him inside a bath towel and called the emergency vet clinic.

"Bring him in. We'll be ready for him."

As I drove toward the animal hospital, my mind buzzed with anxiety. How could this possibly happen? We had already suffered such a loss earlier that year with the passing of Cagney. Money was tight, and I began to imagine how expensive the vet's emergency bill would be. My stomach soured at the thought. I knew we couldn't afford the added expense, especially at Christmastime.

"I need your help here, Lord. We've suffered so much this year with losing Cagney. We can't afford this expensive visit to the vet so would you heal this puppy or take him now and end his suffering?"

In various ways, I continued repeating the prayer, but with the same intent. As I did, the pup began to quiet and eventually slumped. He lay still. Tears streamed down my face as I faced the realization that my new puppy had just died.

I got out of the car. I didn't care that the tears slid down my cheeks, I hurried into the animal hospital. The staff greeted me. The doctor silently took the swaddled dog from my arms and laid him on the counter. Quietly he unwrapped the little guy and to all of our astonishment the puppy sprung up and let out a playful, "Woof!"

"He's alive!" That's all I could say for several seconds.

We looked at one another quizzically before one of the doctors began examining the puppy. "I don't feel anything broken, but we will need to X-ray to get a better assessment and see if there is any internal bleeding."

Two doctors and the nurse scurried to the back and began

working. I talked at length with the receptionist and explained to her the tragedy we had already dealt with earlier that summer and how stretched our finances were. I told her of the events of the evening and how it transpired. Just then the doctor called from the OR. She excused herself and left.

Tension flowed through me. I was certain they had found internal damage and that surgery would be required. I didn't know how we would pay the bill.

The team returned to the front of the office with our newest family member happily licking and nipping at the doctor's hands. Smiles covered the faces of the staff.

"I understand this has been a hard year for your family," the senior doctor said. "Tonight we are part of a real Christmas miracle. Your puppy is living proof. We found no damage."

I took our dog and grinned as I petted him.

"May I ask this little trooper's name?"

"I hadn't gotten that far as we had just arrived home when things went terribly wrong."

"How does the name Lucky sound to you?" He smiled and petted the dog.

The staff members and I laughed heartily. Considering the circumstances of the night, I agreed that was a good name.

"I can't thank you enough for the kindness you have shown me tonight." I still had one more thing to handle. "How much do I owe you?"

"We discussed that in the back room. None of us feel comfortable charging you. It seems that God was the one who did the work on this little fella."

My eyes filled with tears and I thanked them again and hugged each of them. I knew that God had been with us that day: first, by letting my family in out of the cold and now by healing Lucky.

"Merry Christmas and we wish you and your family a much better new year," the receptionist called out as I walked out the door.

That Lucky miracle ended the year on a high note.

33. A Christmas Child

Theresa Robbins with Kathy Winchell

I SQUEEZED DOUG'S HAND AS I SAT ON THE PAPER-COVERED OB-GYN table. It had taken fifteen months for us to conceive. The positive test was an early Christmas gift. Our first appointment was scheduled for twelve weeks. Today, I was five weeks pregnant and cramping.

The doctor entered the room. Just from the way he looked at me, I knew something was wrong.

He leaned against the counter of a stainless-steel sink and boxes of cotton balls. I stared beyond his shoulder at the soft white flakes clinging to the frosted window, unusual for Atlanta, even in December. I waited.

"Your progesterone and HCG levels are extremely low." He cleared his throat and dropped his gaze. "You won't carry to term. I'm sorry."

I didn't want to hear him or to believe his words. He was kind and explained everything, but I really heard nothing except "You won't carry to term."

I left his office in shock. We had tried so hard and Doug and I wanted children. I couldn't get over my grief and sadness.

The rest of December passed in a blur. Christmas came and

went. I remember little of those days. Life as normal continued for others, while I moved robotically through daily activities.

Why, God? Why take my *little one? Why even allow me to get pregnant after all this time if you only intended to take him away?*

"The doctor said we can try again in three months," my husband reminded me.

"Three months?" I shook my head. "We've been down that path before. Three months until we try, but how long before I get pregnant again? Another year?"

Doug sat beside me. He took my hands in his. "We can still adopt."

We had considered adoption, and had even started the process before I got pregnant. I wanted desperately to *bear* a child—his child. An adoptee myself, I hadn't known any of my biological relations. No parents. No siblings. I wanted a blood connection, a boy with my husband's cobalt eyes and strong chin, and a girl with golden curls and my nose.

Once I got past the disappointment and the pain, I realized that most of all I wanted to be a mother. Being a parent was more important to me than continuing to attempt to conceive. I felt free to adopt because I wanted a child.

"Let's call the agency," I said.

Doug smiled and hugged me.

In March, the date the doctor said we could try again, we received a call.

"Congratulations! We have a baby boy who wants to come home with you in August."

Over the next six months, an air of excitement and activity filled our home. We baby-proofed electrical sockets against curious tiny fingers, washed floors and rugs for busy little knees, and purchased all the necessities for our son. We would call him Micah.

As I put together his crib, pasted teddy bear wallpaper, and opened gifts at my baby shower, I felt pregnant. Expectancy and love grew in my heart like a baby swelling in his mother's abdomen.

In August, my skin tingled with anticipation. I expected a call at any moment.

August turned to September. No call.

October was half over before the agency called. "The embassy lost the paperwork. They have to start over again."

"No." I fell into Doug's arms and wailed. "I can't go through this again."

I had heard of adoption "miscarriage." I never understood how it could compare to *my* miscarriage of losing a child from my womb. Now I knew. Would I lose this one, too? I had prayed before; now I prayed even more fervently.

Two months passed with no word from the agency. Doug reminded me what the adoption agency said about the red tape involved in foreign adoptions. My mind understood, but my heart ached. Every day my son stayed in Guatemala, someone else would take care of him. Someone else's arms would hold him when he cried while mine remained empty.

When December came, I didn't think I could bear another childless Christmas. I begged God to bring our baby home. On the evening of December 18, we arrived home after a Christmas party. We listened to a message on the answering machine. The first words were: "It's time to bring home your son."

We flew to Guatemala on December 22. As the plane circled the lush Guatemalan mountains, my heart beat faster. *This is where our son was born and this is where we will finally see him.* At the airport in Guatemala City, we waded through a sea of brown faces. We couldn't find our host. We had no cell phone and no way to contact the agency people. I grew impatient. *Where are they? Did something happen?*

Then I saw him.

A Guatemalan woman who held him squeezed through the crowd and placed him in my arms.

"Micah." Love surged through me. His ebony eyes locked with mine. Could anything on this earth be more beautiful? Tears came to the surface. "Micah," I said again.

Within minutes we climbed into the agency's van and headed for the American Embassy to acquire Micah's final adoption papers. As the van bounced through the city's pitted streets, Micah held our gaze as if he were measuring us. When we reached the embassy, Doug lifted him from the vehicle. Micah instinctively reached out his chubby brown hand and touched Doug's cheek. My composure crumbled; tears poured from the wreckage.

This was our son.

We went through the required procedure at the embassy, which would legally make him ours, but Micah's spontaneous gesture told me that, in his little heart, he already knew.

We flew back to Atlanta on Christmas Eve. Applause and

cheers from friends greeted us at the terminal. Cameras flashed, tears flowed, and WELCOME HOME signs swayed above the crowd. We felt like celebrities. I passed Micah to waiting arms. A reporter thrust a microphone in Doug's face.

"So, how does it feel to bring home your new son on Christmas Eve?"

"It's the best Christmas present we've ever received. A gift from God. No present under the tree can compare."

Later that night, in the quiet of our home, I stared into Micah's crib. I watched his chest rise and fall to his rhythmic breathing. My already saturated heart spilled over in gratitude to God, and I marveled at his timing.

God redeemed last year's Christmas tragedy. He used it to prepare our hearts for adoption because he knew Micah would be waiting for us. God gave me the perfect child—a child not of my blood, but of my heart.

I reverently touched my son's velvety cheek. The hall clock's chime broke midnight's perfect silence. I smiled and whispered to my sleeping son, "Welcome home, my Christmas child."

34. The Miracle of "The Lord's Prayer"

Kelly Carper Palden

AUTUMN 1949, CINDY, MY OLDEST SISTER, WAS TWO YEARS old and the following year, my parents had a son. Life was good for the young farm family in West Bend, Iowa.

A month after David's birth and a few weeks before Thanksgiving, Dad harvested the last of the corn. It was a raw and blustery day. Dad had worked several hours when a neighbor spotted him in the field and flagged him down. The neighbor wanted to return a 12-gauge shotgun that Dad had loaned him during the hunting season. Assuming the gun was being returned unloaded, Dad told him to hang the gun on the tractor's gearshift. After they talked for several minutes, the neighbor drove away.

Alone again in the cornfield, Dad jumped onto the tractor and swung his leg over the seat. His booted foot slammed forcefully into the shotgun and caused it to discharge. The bullet entered his leg just above his five-buckle overshoe and exited just above his bended knee.

Dad knew he should have checked the gun himself; now it was too late. He bled profusely and was more than a mile from home on that cold, windy November day.

Dad was a well-built man, more than six feet tall, and weighed a trim 185 pounds. He had been a star wrestler and football player in high school and college and was used to a tough fight. Tapping into every reserve he had, he determined to survive. With one hand he tried to control the bleeding, while he used the other to unzip his overcoat. He ripped his shirt into strips for bandages.

After he had restricted the blood flow the best he could, Dad crawled down from the tractor seat and unhitched the fully loaded wagon. He might need every ounce of remaining diesel fuel to get home or to locate help. After laboriously lifting himself back onto the tractor, Dad started the engine, gripped the steering wheel, and drove out of the field onto the adjacent gravel road. He hoped he could find someone to help him.

By the time a neighbor saw him, Dad was barely conscious. As the Buick came toward him, Dad pulled the tractor to the edge of the road, and waved and cried out for help.

The neighbor slammed on his brakes. He got out of his car and ran to the tractor. As soon as he realized what happened, he helped my father get off the tractor and into the backseat of the Buick.

He rushed Dad to the nearest hospital. While there, they met another neighbor. He drove to our house to tell Mom.

Years later, Dad told me the story and said, "I held my own in the hospital for almost two weeks before an infection took over." It was probably a staph infection and Dad went into a coma.

By then his sister, a nursing student, took time off from

school to help care for him. She insisted that the hospital transfer Dad to a trauma center in Omaha, which was two hundred miles away.

For nearly a month, Dad was in and out of consciousness. He said he had many dreams. He wasn't able to hear and he couldn't respond to anyone, but something went on inside him. At first, the dreams haunted him about his shotgun ordeal. But over time, a growing number of his dreams were filled with beautiful music and provided great comfort to him.

Besides being an athlete in his younger years, Dad enjoyed playing the violin and singing in the choir or with musical groups. He was the most proud of a 1940s radio recording made of him singing "The Lord's Prayer."

Dad was oblivious of the decision to amputate his right leg just above the knee. The surgery was long and arduous.

Afterward, as he lay heavily sedated in the recovery room, Dad began to sing "The Lord's Prayer" repeatedly. (He wasn't aware of doing that.) The medical staff later told him how beautifully he sang and how much he amazed them with the strength of his voice coming from a seemingly lifeless body. Still unresponsive for several more days, he continued to sing spontaneously from his hospital bed. During his in and out of consciousness time, Dad said that Malotte's "The Lord's Prayer" filled his head and comforted him.

On December 23, at only a few minutes after midnight, Dad regained consciousness. His sister was by his side and Mom arrived soon afterward.

Dad had been only twenty-eight years old at the time of the

accident and took pride in his strong, healthy physique. Now he lay in a hospital bed, missing one leg and trapped in a severely atrophied body. But he was alive. He had a loving wife who had struggled to be at his side while caring for their two young children and overseeing the family's five-hundred-acre farm.

"I was given the best Christmas present of all—my life," he said.

Twelve years later I was born, child number five out of eight siblings. Every Christmas I was able to watch Dad proudly stand in front of the Christmas choir at midnight Mass to sing his traditional solos of "The Lord's Prayer" and "O Holy Night."

Years later, Dad told me that "The Lord's Prayer" had been an incredible comfort to him during those traumatic times, enabling him to fight for his life, and to wake up in time to celebrate Christmas Day with his family.

Throughout his life, Dad demonstrated his conviction of how inner strength can enable a person to persevere through any difficulty in life. Physical therapy hadn't been available at the local hospital. Even if it had been, Dad couldn't afford it, so he rehabilitated himself. He rebuilt his atrophied body, teaching himself to walk and eventually jog on an artificial leg.

Within a few years of his accident, Dad earned a master's degree in agriculture and business economics. He proudly recalled how he walked across campus to classes and crossed the stage on his artificial leg to receive his diploma like everyone else.

Dad became a farm manager, overseeing more than a hundred

farms while tending to his own farmland. He volunteered with the Easter Seals organization, helped to counsel other farm-accident victims, as well as Korean War veterans who had lost a limb. Dad continued to work and vigorously exercise on a daily basis until well into his early eighties.

At Dad's memorial two years ago, my family reflected on his life as we listened to that 1940s recording of him singing his favorite melody. That song will forever bring tears to my eyes and keep pride in my heart for all that Dad accomplished in his life, thanks to his Christmas miracle.

35. One Turbulent Christmas Season

Florence C. Blake

"I'M SICK."

I'd never heard Terry say those words before. My husband had always seemed impervious to illness. That particular Sunday afternoon, however, he coughed occasionally and took an extralong nap on the couch.

I left him alone to rest. But later, when I checked on him, he said, "I'm sick."

I touched his forehead. "It feels too warm. I'm phoning Dr. Robertson's office."

The answering service suggested I take him to the ER, so I drove Terry to Providence Hospital in Medford, Oregon. A staff physician examined him, diagnosed pneumonia, and prescribed an antibiotic. He sent Terry home with, "If you haven't improved by Tuesday, notify Dr. Robertson."

Midday on Tuesday, a few days before Christmas, Terry phoned me at work. He had just seen Dr. Robertson, who had ordered X-rays, and wanted him admitted to Providence Hospital. Terry needed me to drive him there to see the lung specialist, Dr. Blackmon. Before leaving my desk, I called our church.

"Terry is going to Providence Hospital with pneumonia. Please pray."

After Dr. Blackmon examined Terry, he seemed confident. "You have some excess fluid in your lungs. We'll drain that. You should be much better by morning."

I stayed there the rest of the day, kissed Terry good night, and headed home to feed the steers, chickens, and pets on our small ranch.

Before work the next morning, I visited Terry. He didn't look better; he seemed worse. Convincing myself that those things took time, I went to my job.

When I returned to the hospital later, Dr. Blackmon said, "This is one tough strain of pneumonia. We drain one liter from his lungs, and they fill up with two more. We'll drain them again, and strengthen his medication. This may take hours."

God provided neighbors to feed our animals that evening. That allowed me to stay with Terry until after ten thirty on Christmas Eve.

Dr. Blackmon was still there when I left. Terry's case had become such a challenge, his quest for a cure took over. On Christmas Day, the physician and a technician performed another procedure. I sat alone and listened to "White Christmas" through the intercom, and ate a turkey sandwich in an almost-empty cafeteria. Upstairs at Terry's bedside, monitoring his progress on an ultrasound screen, specialists drained still more lung fluid.

"Dear God, please, please help Terry," I prayed. I thought of what a wonderful Christmas present this would be if God would hear my prayer.

By the next morning, the fluid had returned. For several days, Terry remained hospitalized and grew worse. Dr. Blackmon was stumped. Nothing worked. Our church's prayer chains kept busy. Terry's buddy, Rick, visited daily, and walked with him down hospital corridors. It wasn't advisable for pneumonia patients to stay too still for long periods. Nothing improved.

Several days after his hospital admission, my previously cheerful spouse lay silent and didn't respond to me. I went home crying.

Rick phoned me about eleven thirty that night. "What happened?" he asked. "Terry wouldn't get out of bed today, wouldn't walk, and wouldn't talk to me. It's like he doesn't want to fight this anymore."

"I noticed the same thing. He seems to have given up. Please keep praying hard." I hung up the phone, and said another tearful prayer: "Dear God, nothing's too hard for you. Please reverse this horrible condition. Please cure Terry."

Almost immediately, a quiet inner voice spoke to me. *Clean the humidifier.* Where had that thought come from? At first, I rejected the words. I reminded myself that I wiped the humidifier with a soapy dishcloth each time I refilled it. Convinced the message couldn't be from God, I brushed it aside, and continued praying. But I had no peace.

Clean the humidifier.

It still seemed strange to have that thought torment me. Finally, I got up and walked over to my sparkling-clean, styrene appliance. I unplugged it, took it apart, and scrubbed each piece. I aimed a light into the lowest section beneath the water chambers, where overflows spilled.

Then I knew: floating in an inch of water lay a collection of white moldy substances I'd never seen before. "Oh, no!"

Our humidifier had been blowing tainted moisture into the air Terry inhaled while he took midafternoon naps. Old newscasts flashed into my mind. *Legionnaires' disease,* a lethal strain of pneumonia, was originally traced to unsanitary cooling ducts that infected a convention center. Could this be happening in our house?

The next morning, I rushed to Dr. Blackmon as he completed paperwork at the nurse's station. "I'm not medically knowledgeable, so please forgive my ignorance. But might Terry have Legionnaires' disease?"

"No, we ruled out Legionnaires'. He hasn't been in a hotel recently where the system's ductwork might be contaminated—"

"I found an inch of moldy goop floating on the bottom of a humidifier twenty feet from where he naps."

Immediately he went into action. "Take Mr. Blake off that IV and start him on these oral meds," he told the nurse and scribbled new directives. "Get a sputum culture to the lab; tell them we're checking and treating for Legionella bacteria."

When I arrived on the ninth day of Terry's confinement, he was standing up, fully dressed, and smiling. "Hey, gorgeous, they're throwing me out of here. Whatever they did, it worked. Let's go home."

Terry's lab tests had confirmed Legionnaires' disease. Dr.

Blackmon said it had a survival rate of less than 20 percent. But with God's help, we had beaten the odds.

As we walked out of the hospital, I realized that my Christmas present had come a little after Christmas, but it was still the best present I received that season.

36. Baby Jesus Lost

Emily Osburne

THIS IS MY MOM'S STORY, BUT I'VE HEARD IT SO MANY times that I want to tell it as if she wrote this. It has become a special part of our family's Christmas experience.

＊ ※ ＊

"Where is it?" I said aloud. I had looked all through the house. I even searched the attic, under every bed, and behind curtains. In frustration, I tore open a vacuum cleaner bag in search of Jesus. The pieces, made of Italian plastic, were small and the Jesus figure was about the size of my fist. "This is embarrassing. How can I have a crèche without baby Jesus?"

Just then my husband came home. He had gone out to search for a baby Jesus for our crèche. "Please tell me that they had an extra Jesus for sale."

"I don't think this is what you were looking for," Mark said and pulled a figurine out of the shopping bag. "I did my best. The clerk took him out of their manger scene and said that you could return it after the party."

"This baby doesn't match my set." I almost cried as I said, "It's too big."

Mark put the figure back into the shopping bag to return it.

"You don't have time to take it back now." I told him the things he needed to do while I got dressed. Guests would start to arrive within the next half hour. "I want them to see my new wreaths. Make sure the spotlight is centered on the door."

I had spent so much time looking for the figurine I had to rush to get ready. As I hurriedly dressed and put on my makeup, I thought of the family's response when I said I wanted to do everything at our house Christmas Eve. They warned me that I couldn't do it all; I was determined to prove them wrong.

At the time, it hadn't seemed like such a big task. I would host my husband's family for Christmas Eve dinner. The next morning my mother and siblings would arrive for Christmas breakfast. After that, my dad and his wife would join us for lunch. But I still wasn't through because I had volunteered to host a neighborhood party that night.

Ordinarily, I thrived under that kind of pressure. Unable to find the baby Jesus figure, however, had thrown off my timing. But I thought I could pull it off. I had started to prepare weeks earlier. I cooked and froze the things I could, such as the cheese balls, cakes, and mini-quiches.

Christmas week I became my own personal drill sergeant, "Make the fudge, decorate the wreaths, hang the garland, and wrap the gifts," I commanded myself. I ignored my tiredness. "I'll rest after Christmas," I told myself.

Except for the nagging problem of the loss of baby Jesus, I felt a sense of pride. My efforts had paid off. It was the most beautifully decorated our house had ever been. Everything I cooked had turned out just perfect.

It was all coming together. It was beautiful. It was Christmas Eve and it was almost perfect.

"You have really outdone yourself this year, "Aunt Carolyn exclaimed. "Where did you find that gorgeous fresh wreath I saw on your front door?"

"I made the wreath myself. I love fresh greenery, don't you? I stayed up pretty late last night finishing that one." I silently thanked God for strong coffee.

"You have worked so hard, and it's all so gorgeous, but you forgot something." She pointed toward the crèche. "Baby Jesus is missing."

"Oh, no, he's not missing," I lied. "We started a tradition in our family of waiting until Christmas morning to put Jesus in the manger. It is our way of celebrating his birth."

"That's a beautiful ritual. You have really thought of everything."

I felt pangs of guilt because everyone believed my lie and lavished me with praise. To ease my conscience, I decided to turn my little white lie into the truth. The Christmas of 1984 would become the first of many years when we would wait until Christmas morn to put baby Jesus into the crèche. I decided we would first gather around the table and open the Bible to the book of Luke and read about Jesus' birth. Then my two children, Emily and Scott, would gently lay him in his bed and reflect on the true meaning of Christmas. That was the plan and it relieved my guilt for lying.

I went to sleep that night, absolutely exhausted. I didn't stir until Emily jumped up and down in front of my bed.

"Mama, Mama. Wake up! It's time to see what Santa brought."

"Okay, kids. Give your dad one minute to find the camera and then you can start to open presents."

"Mark, what time did you finally get to bed last night?"

"I have no idea. I don't even remember getting to bed."

"I'll make the coffee and you grab the camera." I kissed his cheek. "It's going to be a long day."

It was a long day. The kids loved the presents and the family raved about the fudge. It was a blur of video games, wrapping paper, turkey, and oversized trash bags. After the last neighbor left the house, I wrapped myself inside my new fuzzy robe and fell asleep on the couch.

Mark must have helped me to bed that night, but I don't remember. I awakened the next morning to the familiar aroma of his omelets, and I breathed a sigh of relief that it was all over. I could hear the kids enjoying themselves in the playroom as I started to clean up the mess. It looked like a tornado had come through the house, dropping toys, socks, and Barbie doll clothes everywhere.

I stared at the big wooden toy box that was overflowing with old forgotten toys and decided to clean it out, to make room for new playthings. As I slowly stuffed old dolls and trains into a bag for Goodwill, I spotted something that made me shriek with joy. At the bottom of the toy bin, covered with glitter from Emily's makeup kit, was our little baby Jesus.

Tears welled up in my eyes as I realized that I had forgotten about him. It wasn't just the figurine that slipped my mind. Worse than that, I had completely forgotten the sacredness of the season. I had left Jesus out of Christmas and it was too late to put him back in.

My heart sank as I remembered running around the house, setting the table, washing dishes, opening presents, and leaving cookies for Santa. How did Christmas come and go without even a thought of Jesus? How could I have let that happen?

I pressed the little baby Jesus to my chest, sat in the playroom, and cried. I shook my head, looked up to heaven and whispered, "I will never do it again, Lord. I will never leave you out of Christmas."

I meant it, too. At that moment, something changed inside my heart. The commercialism of the season seemed like rags compared to the true blessing we were supposed to be celebrating. In an instant, I could see myself more clearly. I could see where I had missed the mark. It was time to change. I vowed, "This will be the last Christmas that Jesus gets thrown in the box while our family focuses solely on gifts and goodies."

I am convinced that God allowed baby Jesus to stay hidden until the precise moment that I was ready to see him.

I promised not to lose him again. I never have.

37. Ian's Christmas Gift

Jennifer Lynn Cary

FOR FIVE OF THE SIX CHRISTMASES LEADING UP TO 1998, our son Ian had been in the hospital. From the age of nine, every year it seemed the same. Between his birthday in October and the holidays, we admitted him at least once. Kids with cystic fibrosis have a tough time with weather changes because that's when allergies and RSV (respiratory syncytial virus) kick in.

We'd come to expect those visits and made the most of it. During those Christmas seasons, Ian and I had fun decorating his hospital room and bed. We put mistletoe over his pillow so he could coax nurses into giving him a kiss. They loved it, and he knew it.

In 1997, the hospital released Ian two weeks before Christmas. In my gratitude for the reprieve, I baked and made gifts. I made play dough for my nephews and bread for the neighborhood because I wanted to share our special holiday with everyone. Ian helped me decorate the house, which I hadn't been able to do most of those years. We made seven big ribbon banners—forest green with crimson rosettes—and wrote the words to Isaiah 9:6 in gold across them: "For a child is born to us, a son is given to us. And the government will rest on his shoulders.

And he will be called Wonderful Counselor, Mighty God, Everlasting Father, Prince of Peace." It was a wonderful way to close out the year.

In 1998, Ian seemed healthier than he'd ever been. He'd only had one hospital stay during the preceding twelve months. Because his health thrived, we had family time, a magical oasis where wonderful things came together.

I looked forward to the holidays again. Our daughter, Jaime, would be home from college and once again all our children would be under one roof. My husband, Phil, had received an unexpected inheritance. Like a big kid, he shopped and hid special presents all over the house. He entrusted me to guard one huge box for him. For three weeks, I had to crawl over it to get into bed each night. Phil was so happy for the special Christmas he was able to provide. It was probably the happiest time our family had enjoyed in years.

About ten days before Christmas, when I came home from work Ian was seated on the kitchen counter next to the phone. He watched the TV in the living room and clutched the telephone to his ear.

"What are you doing?"

"I'm trying to win that contest." He pointed at the television. "It's a family pack to the IMAX Theater to see *The Nutcracker*."

"Oh." I nodded and put away my things.

"It's going to be my Christmas present to the family," Ian said. "I don't want to spend my money because I want to go visit Jaime at school next spring."

That was important to him. He'd e-mailed her and a few of her friends who thought he was cute with his big eyes, adorable freckles, and impish grin. He was fifteen, and I wasn't about to burst his bubble about college girls. "Sweetie, just don't be too disappointed if you can't get—"

His hand went up. "Yes, my name is Ian." After a pause, he yelled, "Cool!" He turned toward me and gave me his I-told-you-so look.

I responded with a thumbs-up and let him finish his call.

Ian won the family pack. He took us to see *The Nutcracker*. We wore 3-D viewers to get the full impact of the IMAX. It felt strange watching decorations and shapes fly past my head, knowing they really were just up on the screen.

"Whoa, did you see that, Mom?" He leaned over and whispered the first time.

"See it? I ducked!" The special effects impressed all of us.

Ian beamed with excitement because he was able to give us that as his gift. As we left the IMAX, he asked, "So, did you like it?"

"Yes, sweetie, I did, very much." I brushed my thumb over his cheek, seeing part boy and part promise of the man to be. A fierce desire to stop time and hold on to this moment washed over me.

✳ ✳ ✳

Christmas morning my husband shook me. "It's time to wake up." I usually had to coerce him out of bed.

"What time is it?" I pulled my pillow closer. We'd earned that bonus of sleeping in now that our kids were older.

"Come on, get up. You know you want to."

"It took me forever to get the kids old enough to sleep in on Christmas morning. What are you doing?" Cold air breezed up my gown as he yanked the covers back. I gave in and felt around for my glasses.

"Help me wake the kids."

"Wake them yourself," I grumbled and wandered into the living room to curl up in the corner of the couch.

A fire blazed in the fireplace, and coffee dripped rhythmically into the pot in the kitchen. The aroma of cinnamon rolls wafted throughout the house. When did he make those? A giant bow graced the cabinet where the TV sat hidden from view, suspiciously concealing behind the doors what I knew to be a new set.

I have no recollection of the material gifts received that Christmas morning. Most of them are probably gone, used up, broken, or given away. Our being together, laughing, teasing, and hugging is what stands out in my memory. My mind can still scan the room and picture the smiles and listen to the interaction. *We were together.* That was enough to make me content.

That day, my heart overflowed with an indescribable sense of love. God had given us a Christmas to rest. After six years of December trips to the hospital, we finally celebrated the birth of our Savior with gratitude for an extraspecial gift, a peaceful holy season all together.

I didn't know it then, of course, but that would be our last Christmas together. Five months later Ian died.

Our girls have grown up and moved to places of their own.

Sometimes Phil and I go away for Christmas and sometimes we stay home. I don't decorate as much now. Even the Isaiah ribbons stayed in their box this past year. It can get too hard.

"Christmas isn't the same," I say to myself. "How could it be?" I still miss Ian, but I've learned to pause, thank God for the years we were together, and focus on the true meaning of the day. I try to forget the hustle and material things that won't last as life goes on. That helps.

But each Christmas, I have a little trick I do. If I close my eyes just right, I can see Ian sitting on the counter, phone in hand. He gives me a thumbs-up.

I smile, give him a thumbs-up, and wish him a Merry Christmas.

38. A Christmas Healing

Ingrid Briles

"THERE'S BEEN AN ACCIDENT," THE POLICE OFFICER SAID. "Come quickly!"

The cruiser waited for me in front of the restaurant where I worked. I remained in such shock I remembered little of the drive. It sunk in that my daughter had been struck by a car. When we hurried to the hospital, I was vaguely aware of the officer saying to a nurse, "This is the mother."

Someone took me to the family room. Immediately I saw my former mother-in-law, who worked for the head of orthopedic medicine. She had been notified as soon as the trauma team had been contacted.

A nurse handed me forms for blood transfusions, X-rays, abdominal surgery, orthopedic surgery, and a CT scan. When I read the consent form for emergency neurosurgery, I couldn't sign my name. I stood there, unable to do anything. About that time, her dad came into the family room and signed the forms.

My child went from a chattering, bubbling six-year-old who had been excited about school to a comatose little girl lying in a bed too big for her. The long, thick blond hair that bounced along behind her had been shaved for neurosurgery. Legs that ran and played hopscotch were held by traction, trying to re-connect breaks in her femurs.

She was too injured to survive. The machines went silent and so did my soul.

We buried her on a mountain that overlooks West Virginia's Kanawha River. After the funeral, her dad went his way. Our son lost his little sister to an auto accident; he lost his dad to depression.

He lost me to a bottle. I never drank much before then; after that, I couldn't stop.

My former in-laws took my son. At the time, it was one more reason to be hurt and angry. It was another reason to drink: I had lost my daughter and they had taken my son.

After that, I couldn't bring myself to drive past the accident site on my way to work. The cemetery seemed to call me to join my child and I thought of suicide many times. I quit my job and left the state.

In my new location, I found a job. After that, all my days seemed the same. I went to work, came home, and ate (some-times), got drunk, passed out, and awakened the next morning to start another bleak, empty day.

One day it rained—a cold, gray day. I walked to work in my usual state of depression and anger and I was also hungover—another usual condition. Without warning, a cloud burst and a heavy rain struck. I had nowhere to hide, no raincoat, and no umbrella. Within minutes, I was soaked.

I was furious. I looked toward the heavens, shook my fist, and shrieked, "Is there anything else you can do to me?"

Almost as if God heard me and spoke, something happened. I had been raised in the church but after my daughter's death, I hadn't gone back. Just then, with my eyes opened, as strange as it may seem, I saw Jesus on the cross. In that moment, God was no longer the powerful, impersonal, angry one. He was a father and it must have broken his heart to watch them torture his son and murder him. In an unexplainable way, I felt God touch my soul. I don't know if I really heard his voice, but these words softly filled my mind: "I understand. My child died, too."

In the pouring rain, I sat on the curb and bawled. I didn't care if anyone saw me; I didn't care what anyone thought. I cried until no more tears flowed. I cried for my dead daughter. I cried for my son who had suffered without parents to comfort him.

And I cried for myself.

Then I stopped crying. It was as if I had shed all the tears I needed to let go of the pain of the past. With a calmness I hadn't felt for a long time, I got up and walked home in the rain. I called the restaurant and quit my job.

A few days later I drove back to West Virginia. As I drove, I understood that God could have protected his own son, but he had let him go. I released my bitterness and my pain. I let my daughter go.

When I got back to West Virginia, a verse from the Bible ran through my mind. Jesus said, "But when you are praying, first forgive anyone you are holding a grudge against, so that your Father in heaven will forgive you your sins, too" (Mark 11:25).

I called the woman who had driven the car that day. I had screamed at her and said terrible things. I asked her to forgive my terrible treatment of her after the accident. "It was no one's fault," I said. "It was just a tragic accident." As I spoke those words, I knew they were true.

Something happened to me in the middle of that thunderstorm and I became different. I found a place to live and within days I had a job. I had no desire to drink. I went back to church. I contacted my son, asked him to forgive me, and he did.

Christmas came—and for five years I hadn't been able to go into stores filled with dolls and dresses. I couldn't go to the mall and watch little girls sit on Santa's lap. I hadn't celebrated Christmas since her death. During that five-year period, I hadn't sent my son a gift or even a card.

Now, sober, back home, and rebuilding a relationship with my son, I tried to go to the mall, and it was still something that I couldn't do.

On impulse, I called a local church and asked the pastor if they had a family who needed help for the holidays. He told me about one family and they had asked for just one thing: They wanted gifts for their only daughter. She was six years old and going into second grade.

I joyfully agreed to provide gifts for her. To my amazement, she wore my daughter's sizes, liked the same colors, and shared the same favorite toys she had at that age. I went boldly to the mall. I was excited to help the needy child, but I felt a sense of closure for myself. *I'm shopping one more time for my daughter.*

I walked through the stores, bought dolls, Care Bears, dresses, and everything that I would have bought for my own daughter. After that, I shopped for my son. He would receive Christmas presents from me for the first time in five years.

As I moved from store to store, I listened to the Christmas music. I smiled at the bright lights and decorations. This is a wonderful, wonderful Christmas, I thought, and I allowed the words of the carols to fill my soul.

Once I was home, I stared at the face of the stranger in my bathroom mirror. She smiled back at me. It had been a long, long time since I had seen her smile.

I took the gifts to the church and asked the pastor not to give my name. The next morning, while praying, I felt what I call "a shower of blessing" descend on me. I knew without doubt that the little girl's parents were praying for me and thanking God for me.

My healing was complete.

Since that Christmas, my son and I have developed a loving relationship. God has blessed him with a wonderful wife, and soon his first child will be born.

In the years that have passed, I joyfully shop for Christmas but always, my first gift is for my daughter. I lovingly buy gifts that I can give to someone else. Sometimes God allows my memory of her to bless a little boy and other years the gift goes to a little girl. One year the child is her age, and at other times older or younger. The child may be of our race, but not every year. It doesn't matter. This is my gift to the world in honor of my beloved daughter.

This past Christmas as I thought again of the healing miracle in my life, I also thought of a story in the Bible. After King David's infant son died, he said, "He can't return to me, but someday, I will go to him."

And so it is with me.

39. A Light in the Closet

Renie Burghardt

I WAS BORN IN THE BÁCSKA REGION OF HUNGARY. BÁCSKA IS on the Serbian border, where both Hungarians and Serbians lived. In 1944, as World War II intensified and Tito's communist partisans began closing in on the region, my grandparents, who raised me, decided that we should leave our home and move to a safer area.

One morning in early fall, we left the region in my grandfather's horse-drawn wooden wagon. We packed some of our belongings, but left behind most things that had been familiar and dear.

On our journey we met people in hundreds of other wagons on the road. Like us, they sought a safer place.

"But where are the safe places?" my grandmother asked.

My grandfather didn't try to answer. He continued to drive away from our home. We went along that way for several days.

Sometimes someone would hear warplanes in the distance. "Planes!" a voice would shout.

Everyone stopped and we jumped from our wagons. All of us ran toward the nearest ditch. We never knew when those planes would drop bombs or strafe us. We had endured both.

At dark, everyone stopped and camped on the side of the road. We built small fires, ready to extinguish them if planes came. They rarely bombed at night so it was usually safe. We cooked and ate our meager suppers before we went to sleep in our wagons.

We finally settled in a city named Zirc. My grandparents thought we were in a safe area. Christmas that year was meager, but we celebrated it with a tiny tree and handmade gifts. However, the day after Christmas, warplanes approached the city. Sirens filled the air, followed minutes later by the deafening explosion of bombs, and our house began to shake.

"The closet! Run into the closet!" It wasn't an audible voice, but it was so strong, I didn't question its source. Terror-stricken, I ran toward the closet. "Come!" I shouted at the others.

My frightened grandparents followed. Inside the closet, I sank down into a corner and covered my ears with my hands to shut out the deafening noises. I closed my eyes so I wouldn't have to see anything. My grandfather pulled the closet door shut.

"Sweetheart, everything will be all right," my grandmother said. She pulled me into her arms.

The house shook and I could hear everything crumbling around us. My body shook with fear and I must have screamed. Pieces of rubble and dust fell from the ceiling.

"I can't breathe," I cried out. "And it's dark in here."

"It's all right," my grandmother said.

"I'm so scared. Are we going to die?"

"Pray, sweetheart, pray. God will protect us," Grandma said

and held me tightly while Grandfather shielded us with his own body.

"Dear God, I'm so scared, and I can't breathe good. It is so dark in here. Please help us. Please, God . . ." my voice trailed off. I was on the verge of losing consciousness. I closed my eyes again. Just then, I felt a soothing touch caress my face. I opened my eyes to a shimmering light in front of me. I reached out toward the light to touch it. I couldn't touch it, but it made me feel calm. My breathing moderated. Fear slipped away.

The bombing ceased. We had no idea how long we stayed there, but we were alive.

"Grandma, do you see the light?" I pointed to the door. "It is so beautiful." It was a white light, like a glow. I tried to describe it.

"No, I don't see it. But I hear something." Her arms were still around me.

Much later that morning Grandfather moved. "There are people out there," he said. "I hear them." He leaned against the closet door. He beat against the door and yelled, "We're in here! We're alive!" He pushed on the door, but debris that had fallen inside stopped him. Outside, the door was blocked, but we yelled and pounded.

Within minutes, the diggers got to us and dug away the rubble that held us prisoner. They finally pulled us out of the closet.

Once we were outside, we heard about our neighbors. Many of them had died in the bombing.

Miraculously, the closet itself had stayed mostly intact beneath the rubble, and because we were in it, our lives were saved.

"What made you run into the closet?" my grandmother asked later.

"I heard a voice. It told me to run into the closet," I said. I also told them about the light that took away my fear.

"Thank you, God," Grandfather prayed.

"Your guardian angel was looking out for you," Grandmother said and stroked my face, "and he will continue to do so, don't ever forget that."

We had had a meager Christmas that year and for more years following. Sadness had filled my heart, but I can never forget that night in the closet. I believe it was God's angel that told me to run into the closet. That same invisible angel soothed my frightened soul.

And to this day, whenever I'm afraid of something, I know there is a light in some closet, waiting for me to flee to it.

40. Pray and Trust

Drienie Hattingh

"I'm in trouble and I'm not sure what to do. Amy and I argued and she stormed off, leaving me alone."

"What happened?" I tried to keep the panic out of my voice.

Brenda phoned from Barcelona. "I can't believe this, I'm in a strange land and I can't speak the language. Amy took the Spanish dictionary, the map, and the address of the hostel where we're supposed to stay." Brenda sounded more angry than scared.

This was supposed to have been a special trip for her. After working as a waitress and saving money for a summer, Brenda took a year's break from college and accompanied twenty other students on the University of Minnesota's Study in England program.

I had waved good-bye to her when she went through customs at the airport, but I had been concerned, maybe even slightly worried: Brenda had never been that far away from her family. We'd attended the orientation program and met the college instructors who would chaperone the students, but I still worried. Maybe I was just being the fearful mother.

I had gotten past my worries when she called from England

to say that she had an opportunity to stay over the Christmas holiday period and see more of Europe. She and another student, Amy, decided to use their one-week Christmas holiday to travel by train to Spain and stay at youth hostels. I felt uneasy again, but Brenda assured me that many students did that. "We'll be fine," she said.

My husband, Johan, our youngest daughter, Yolandi, and I decided to spend our Christmas holidays traveling through Arizona. We kept in touch with Brenda by leaving messages for each other on our home phone. We left phone numbers for the hotels where we stayed on our answering machine. She promised to call us every day, tell us where she was, and that would assure us that she was all right.

At midnight, four days before Christmas, while we were in Sedona, Arizona, we received the distress call from Brenda. She called from a little café in Barcelona, Spain, and told us about her argument with Amy.

I listened in horror and my heart beat furiously. "What are you going to do?" I envisioned my child standing in the café, with her enormous backpack that was much too large for her small frame, her big brown eyes full of frustration, and surrounded by strangers who spoke in a foreign language.

"I'm going to look for a police officer," she said. She apologized for upsetting me. "Don't worry. I'll communicate somehow and ask for directions to a hostel or something. I've still got the whole day ahead of me to find a place to stay tonight."

"What if no one understands you?"

"I'll be fine, don't worry, Mom." The line went silent.

I felt numb. Her last words echoed in my mind, "Don't worry, Mom." I felt absolutely frustrated in the hotel room with the useless receiver in my hand. I wanted to beg her to return to London but I couldn't call the number back and there was no one else I could call. If something went wrong, we wouldn't know. Worse, no one would know where to go look for her.

A terrible night followed in which I worried and hardly slept. I kept praying for God to let Brenda find someone who would understand her and that she would find a safe place to sleep. The next two days we called home many times, but there were no messages from Brenda. We continued to call, and each time we left our phone number on the answering machine. Why didn't she call us or leave a message on our home phone, as we had arranged? Granted, we were traveling from hotel to hotel, but we left contact information for her.

Two days before Christmas we checked into another hotel. The first thing I did was to ask the receptionist if there were any messages for us.

"No messages," the clerk said.

We registered, and as we walked through the lobby to the elevator, Yolandi pointed excitedly to the huge, glittery Christmas tree. "Look at the angel. Isn't she beautiful?"

The angel was lovely. She had a serene, comforting smile on her face and her arms were extended, as though to assure us that she was watching over us. She reminded me of a picture from childhood of a guardian angel, who hovered over two small children as they crossed a dangerous bridge with a raging river below.

I didn't sleep that night. I kept on praying, asking God to keep his hand over Brenda. As I prayed, I "saw" the Christmas angel in the hotel's lobby. A few months earlier at a Bible study at our church we had talked about angels. The lessons emphasized that they are God's ministering spirits and come among us when needed. I asked God to send his angels to watch over Brenda. However, visions of everything that could go wrong kept going through my mind. I lay awake and when the first rays of morning filtered into the room, I still hadn't slept.

"Do you believe in prayer?" Johan asked when he saw the state I was in.

"Yes," I said. "You know I do."

"If you believe in praying, you have to pray and then trust."

Johan was right. I had prayed, but acted as if God hadn't heard me. I had to learn to trust God. The rest of the day, whenever I thought of horrible things that could happen to Brenda, I envisioned angels hovering over my child, keeping her out of danger.

On Christmas Eve, we called home. Brenda had left us a message.

"Mom! Dad! Where are you? I keep missing you at hotels. Wish you could be here. Especially you, Mom. It's beautiful! The ancient buildings, the ambiance, the little shops, the people, you would have loved it. And guess what? I ran into Amy today on the beach. We're friends again, so everything is fine. Don't worry anymore. Oh, and have a wonderful Christmas!"

I was so relieved, I cried in Johan's arms. It was as if a burden was lifted off my shoulders and I thanked God repeatedly for sending his angels to watch over Brenda.

Only after Brenda returned from England did I learn how thoroughly God had answered my prayers.

After the connection was broken between us on that frightening night in Arizona, Brenda wandered around the beautiful city all day. Even though she was lost and alone, she enjoyed her amazing surroundings. She saw two women standing on a street corner ahead. As she came closer, she heard them speaking in Afrikaans—*our native language.*

Overcome with relief, she greeted them. After hearing of her predicament, they hugged her and invited her to stay with them at a convent.

A convent. I could not believe my ears when Brenda told me. The nuns welcomed her and fussed over her. They gave her a bed and fed her. When she went out exploring the city, they gave her their phone number. "They even waited up for me that night," Brenda said.

God not only sent angels to comfort Brenda when she was lost and alone, he sent angels who spoke her native language. Angels in the form of nuns to take care of my little girl, just as I would have done.

I often think of that Christmas angel we observed in the hotel lobby. I believe God tried to speak to me through the angel Yolandi pointed out. Not only did he take care of my daughter, but he taught me an important lesson: "Pray and trust."

41. Stretching Christmas

Mary Kay Moody

THE FLAME ON THE STOVE FLICKERED AND WENT OUT. THAT was the last of the propane. I tasted the chili. It was only luke-warm, but there was nothing more I could do.

Six-year-old Karl walked into the kitchen with a half-filled grocery sack. "Done, Mom."

I smiled at his tenderness. Despite our own reduced circumstances, my son had packed several of his toys to donate to less fortunate kids who might not receive Christmas gifts. "Wash your hands. Dinner's ready." I put the chili on the table with crackers and a jar of peanut butter.

We prayed and thanked God for the food we had. After I finished, Karl started to eat. Instead of eating, I silently prayed, *God, please show me what to do.* I thought of a place in Proverbs that reads, "Trust in the LORD with all your heart; do not depend on your own understanding. Seek his will in all you do, and he will show you which path to take" (3:5–6).

"This is good, Mom." Karl paused, looked up, and smiled.

The Bible says to trust you and not follow my own understanding. I don't know how to do that. What should I do? What can I do? I'm low on money. I can't even provide for my son. I feel so lost. Would you put some kind of light on the right road sign?

"It's real good chili."

"Thanks, honey."

He finished eating and said, "I'm cold."

The howling December-in-Chicago winds made me wonder how long before the temperature in our trailer dipped below freezing. "Grab your heavy sweatshirt. We don't have any more propane."

I bundled Karl inside his parka and we played checkers. About ten minutes later the phone rang.

It was my friend Linda who called. "I just got home. Can you two come over for dinner?"

"Sorry, but we ate early tonight."

"And I'm late. The sudden cold wave really slowed the buses. How about coming over for tea or cocoa?"

I ached to say yes, for even an hour of warmth. But I knew if we were going to sleep through this icy night, we needed to crawl into bed before the cold chilled too deeply. "I'd better not tonight. I'm putting Karl to bed—"

"It isn't even seven o'clock. Is he sick?"

"No, he's not sick." I blew a breath over my chilly nose. I hated to tell Linda the truth. She had rescued us last month, and even bought fifty dollars worth of propane.

"What's wrong?"

Finally I told her our plan to sleep in parkas and under every blanket we owned.

"You're not staying there. You're going to sleep here tonight." She lived in a trailer down the street from ours. When I protested that she had done so much for us already, she brushed that aside. "Come. Now."

I finally agreed. We grabbed clothes and toothbrushes, and minutes later, we sat in her warm kitchen and sipped cocoa. Elegant porcelain dolls, trailing ivy, and Christmas decorations filled the living room. I felt almost as if I were in an English manor.

I thanked her profusely several times. She had proven to be a special friend to Karl and me.

She leaned forward, took my hand, and said, "Tomorrow, go to the township office. They'll get you propane."

"Even though I work part time?"

"You can't afford to fill your tank, so yes, I think they will." She slid her door key across the table. "Take this. If you can't get fuel tomorrow, come back here. I should be home by six."

I thanked her, but I left the key on the table. I hated to admit that we needed it. "When I quit waitressing, I thought finding another job would be easy. Always has been."

"You did what you believed God told you to do."

I had changed many things in my life. I had undergone a conversion experience and become active in church. I quit my waitress job because I had to push alcohol, which brought in more money than the food. In the afternoons, I had also run the bar. After I became a serious Christian, I didn't feel right doing that.

I had studied real estate and passed the state exam. In one

afternoon I went from steady income to being "on commission." Mortgage rates were 13 percent, but the realtors' training provided good information, contacts, and rationale why people should still buy homes.

I called people, answered the office phones, took wide-eyed young couples out looking. *I sold nothing.* By winter, interest rates soared beyond 20 percent. I listed a house, but it hadn't sold. Until it did, I'd earn nothing. I took a part-time job as a waitress at a deli. The work there was fine, but it wasn't enough. I had to choose food and gasoline or heat for my rented trailer.

That night Linda hugged me and shuffled off to bed. She would leave for work while it was still dark. I stayed at the table and sipped tea. As I watched steam rise from my teacup, I wondered how I could provide a joyful Christmas for Karl. *God, he's so young. I don't mind for myself but help me provide a special Christmas for him. I know you haven't stopped loving us. Please show me.*

After I finished my tea, I walked to the spare bedroom. As I got into bed, the wind shrieked around the corners of the trailers. As discouraged as I was, I thanked God for the warm bed. I had committed myself to trust God. I had no sense that anything would change, and yet I went to sleep at peace.

The next day I did exactly as Linda told me. I sat across from a thin, quick-moving woman at the township office. I explained my situation, filled in the forms, and waited.

She scanned the documents. "What fuel company do you use?"

"Gee Brothers."

She lifted her phone, punched numbers, and ordered me 150 gallons of propane. "They'll bill our office," she said.

"Bill your office?" I was shocked and overwhelmed with gratitude to God. I silently thanked God repeatedly. I gathered my papers, and stood to leave.

"Wait."

I sat down. *I suppose she wants to know when I can pay for the propane.*

"What about food? Do you have enough?"

I ticked off items in my mind. "I have enough for about three days."

She dug through a drawer. "Where do you typically shop?"

"Eagle Foods."

She pulled out what looked like a receipt book, wrote something, ripped out a coupon, and passed it to me. "Here's a store credit for fifty dollars."

I bit my lips to restrain the tears. *This will buy a lot of chili, tuna, and peanut butter.* "Thank you, thank you," I said. "You have no idea—"

She smiled and said, "Merry Christmas. And good luck job-hunting."

With careful list-making, I was able to buy enough food for at least three weeks. But the special joy was that Karl and I could *do* Christmas. We bought baking supplies, and over the next week we laughed and sang as we stirred nut breads and cookie dough. I did the measuring, Karl, the frosting and sprinkles. We were excited that we would be able to give away most of our homemade Christmas goodies.

After I tucked Karl into bed, I thanked God for everything and for a warm trailer. "Just one more thing, Lord. I've tried to be careful with the money and we've shared our bounty with others. But I don't have anything for Karl. I can't even afford to buy him a toy." I wiped away my tears as I thought, *Karl loves to make things for others and to share what he has. He's so giving. Please God, just—just something.* Karl wanted a Stretch Armstrong. That wasn't possible, but he would be happy with any toy.

Every cent I earned at the deli I stashed inside an envelope for next month's rent, gas for the car, and for heat. Much as I ached to take twenty dollars to buy the toy he wanted, I couldn't. "I have to take the responsible road," I said aloud.

One mid-December afternoon, I sipped a cup of tea and opened the mail. One letter came from my widowed aunt, Kitty, who lived across the country. I had seen her perhaps half-a-dozen times growing up. She had never sent birthday cards or Christmas presents. But this year, she sent a Christmas card. "That was nice of her," I said.

As I opened the card to read it, a check dropped into my lap. She had sent us a Christmas check for twenty-five dollars.

I cried for several minutes. God had performed a miracle. Never once in my life had Aunt Kitty ever sent me a gift. Why this year? I asked myself, but I knew the answer. "I know this has to be your guidance," I told God.

Christmas morning Karl shrieked with joy after he opened his squishy, stretchy doll.

As he played with his toy, I thought of Aunt Kitty. She didn't believe in God. But I smiled. She might not believe, but God used her to bring us a miracle for Christmas. God also reminded me that he provides miracles to take care of us when we need it.

42. A Little Angel's Big Prayer

Phyllis Ring

MOM HAD DIED. I KNEW THAT AS SOON AS I HEARD DAD'S voice on the answering machine. She had been so sick that my sister and I felt it was God's reprieve.

We handled her death and the funeral as well as any two loving daughters could have. But Dad seemed encased in a mountain of ice as he roamed through the house in sad-faced silence. After sixty years of marriage, he couldn't visualize life without her. Worse, he didn't seem to want to try.

After all the family members went home, I stayed with Dad for a week. The depressive sadness didn't leave, but he assured me he would be all right. He lasted six days on his own and collapsed.

My sister took him to her house, midway between where Dad lived in Florida and our home in New Hampshire. He was admitted to a local hospital for gall bladder surgery that turned out to be gangrenous, which explained why he'd become so sick.

For the second time in three weeks, I boarded a plane.

His appearance appalled me. He didn't seem to care whether he lived or died. We wanted him to fight to live. We were afraid he would give up. Daily and fervently I begged God to encourage him and to make him want to live.

Instead of improving, Dad became increasingly unresponsive. As I visited him, no matter how hard I tried to push it away, discouragement came over me.

Christmas Eve I asked God to help me do what I could for Dad. I hadn't wanted him to die, of course, but finally I prayed for God's will to be done. After he had spent two weeks in the hospital, I could hardly go each day and see his sad, depressed face. With each visit, he seemed to have gone a little further downhill.

I had to force myself to visit the hospital Christmas morning, but I went. As I walked toward his room I thought, *This might be the last time I'll ever see him alive.*

I went into the room and to my surprise, Dad was sitting up in bed. He smiled—that warm, loving smile I hadn't seen since before Mom died. "I walked this morning," he called out. "Not once but twice."

I hugged him, delighted at the news and more delighted at his change of attitude.

"I've got to get out of here," he said and I marveled at the brightness of his eyes.

Before I could ask what happened, Dad said, "Your mother sent a little angel last night. He told me that's what God wants me to do—to get up and go on with my life."

"Little angel?" I asked. I wondered if the drugs had caused him to hallucinate.

"Yes, a special little angel." He smiled. He told me about a phone call from a friend of our family named Di. "She called to wish me a happy Christmas even though I was in this bed." He went on to say that she told him about her five-year-old nephew, Tristan. Apparently she and the boy talked regularly about God.

"Tristan visited me Sunday," she told Dad, "and we found a scraggly branch, stuck it in the snow, and made a Charlie Brown Christmas tree. As we decorated it, he looked at me and asked, 'Auntie Di, are you okay?' I told him I've been worried about my friend." Di explained to the boy, "Phyllis's mummy died, and her daddy's been so sad. Nobody knows what to do for him."

According to Di, the boy paused as if absorbing the information before he said, "Of *course* the daddy's sad. The mummy died!"

Tears filled Di's eyes and she hugged him.

"But God can make anything better, Auntie Di. And tomorrow's special because it's Jesus' birthday. I'm going to ask God to tell the daddy that the mummy is with Jesus, and that everything is going to be okay."

After Dad finished telling me the story, he smiled again. "And it *is* going to be okay."

The day after Christmas, Dad left the hospital. He wasn't the same man who had gone in. The sadness had lifted. Joy and peace filled his heart.

I'll long remember that event. Tristan was God's special angel, sent to Dad, even though he touched him secondhandedly. God honored that child's faith and Dad had the joy of being touched by a little angel's big prayer.

43. "Do Not Worry"

Denise Aulie

"COME SEE, SEÑORA! YOU HAVE TO COME SEE!" A FIST pounded against our metal gate in the small Mexican town where our family lived.

I ran to the gate.

Juan pointed to the south. "Look!"

Popocatépetl, the volcano that I had looked at through my window for years, had started to erupt. We lived in a town called San Mateo Cuanala in the state of Puebla, about twenty miles from the volcano.

I stood mesmerized by the flashing lights reflected across the sky. Smoke, fire, and red lava careened down the slopes toward the villages. "Juan! People live along the path of the volcano! Can they escape in time?"

Later we learned that a man named Francisco, who lived in the village below the erupting path, heard the rumbling. He did nothing until the foundation of his adobe home began to shake. He gathered his family in his truck and drove away. He remembered my husband, Eduardo, who had visited him years before to buy wood to build our home. My husband had played with the children and talked to them about God's love. Because of that, Francisco knew where he could take his family.

After Francisco drove up to our gate, we asked about his home and others in the pathway of the volcano. Instead of answering, he motioned for us to follow him to his truck. A tarp covered the rickety wooden sides. He threw back the covering. Inside were thirty people—men, women, and children—and one lamb. Not one of them made a sound. They stared at us, but their faces seemed to plead with us for help.

"This is my family," Francisco said. "They are my cousins, my aunts, uncles, and a few neighbors."

Eduardo didn't hesitate. He turned to me. "What would you say if we took them in until this volcano thing blows over?"

Before I could answer, Francisco yelled to them in Spanish, "Everyone get out!"

Noisily and hurriedly, the stronger and younger ones jumped to the ground and helped the older, weaker ones.

I stared at them. I wanted to help them but where could I put thirty homeless people this Christmas?

As if I had spoken aloud, Francisco pointed to deteriorating brick-built rooms where we had lived before we built our house.

My husband nodded his approval. Francisco organized them and everyone seemed to have a task. Some swept the building; others gathered firewood. Before long, outdoor cooking fires provided warmth and it was obvious the women were ready to cook.

We had to provide the food for them, of course. But how could we? What would we feed them? And would there be enough old trees to provide heat for them at night? Where would they get enough drinking water?

All kinds of practical questions troubled me, from needing rolls of toilet paper to getting mats for them to sleep on. How much food would we need? And for how long?

None of us had any idea how long it would be before they could return and rebuild their homes. As I watched them cleaning up and excitedly making the best of an old building, I wondered how long we'd have to take care of them.

Just then, I thought of the words of Jesus: "I tell you not to worry about everyday life—whether you have enough food and drink, or enough clothes to wear. Isn't life more than food, and your body more than clothing? Look at the birds. They don't plant or harvest or store food in barns, for your heavenly Father feeds them. And aren't you more valuable to him than they are?" (Matthew 6:25–26).

I'd read those words many times but hadn't thought about them a great deal. This would be a test of my faith and my obedience to what I said I believed.

We shared what food we had and it seemed to be enough. We made it through the first night with blankets on cement floors for warmth. Families huddled together to sleep. The next morning, I went from person to person pouring them hot coffee.

I stared at the people. I was sure there had been only thirty people, but as I looked around, I was certain that there must be twice that number. Each of them looked up at me and smiled.

"Last night about thirty-five more relatives arrived," Francisco said. "We didn't want to wake you. Not to worry. We told them that you believed in God and that we would all be taken care of because of God."

What could I say to that?

Just then, my teenage daughter, Alexa, came up to me. "Don't worry, Mom. I'll find help for us." She decided to go to all of our neighbors and ask for help for the "volcano people."

Our neighbors responded. As others heard, they sent food, clothing, and cooking utensils. Even a drug rehab center sent gifts from their meager resources. The person who brought food and clothes from the center said, "We know what it is like to be in need."

Compassionate doctors set up a clinic in our front room. A young family, who had produced a bumper crop of blue corn, sent burlap bags of corn. I witnessed the constant making of tortillas by the displaced women and they smiled and laughed the entire time. Some people we hardly knew came, bringing thirty small mattresses and blankets.

With the help of others we had bikes, soccer balls, and other playground equipment.

Despite the deprivation our visitors endured, they seemed to be filled with a joyous spirit of gratitude.

Just before Christmas Eve, I didn't know what to do. I hoped for some kind of traditional festive meal, but that seemed impossible. I mentioned it to my family.

Alexa again spoke out, "Don't worry." She and her teenage friends went out again. They found a warm-hearted business-woman who supplied a complete, colorful Christmas meal. We even had the traditional Christmas punch prepared by a kind chef.

My biggest surprise is that we had leftover food. I had worried about not having enough. God had touched hearts of people who provided with abundance. It was almost like the miracle of the feeding of the five thousand in the Bible. Except God used people to provide for the multitude.

Christmas Day, as soon as we finished eating on donated tables that dotted the whole yard, Eduardo stood up and opened his Bible. A hush came over the crowd. My husband spoke to them about God loving us and providing for us. He brought out the Christmas message of Jesus coming into the world as a man to save humanity. "Jesus didn't have a home here on earth," he said. He applied that to them and went on to say how God had provided for them.

I don't know what went on inside their hearts and minds, but I think they grasped the reality that God provided for them in their great time of need.

After Eduardo finished, someone brought in colorful piñatas and we watched the children playing.

A few minutes later, Francisco came up to my husband and me. "You saw the lamb we brought with us?"

I nodded.

"We ask you to receive the lamb as a humble gift—truly the only gift we have to give. Allow us to give that lamb to prepare a meal for you because this Christmas you gave all of us a home when we could not be in our own."

Through my tears I nodded. I think my husband's eyes teared up as well.

Somehow—and I couldn't begin to explain how—we were able to provide for those sixty-five people for three weeks. After that, the Mexican government gave them permission to return home. My eyes misted again the day they left. They carried back donated clothes, food, blankets, and mattresses. The government provided trucks for them. As they drove away, they called out thanks and waved.

I cried with sadness to see them leave; I cried with joy because Jesus had done for us exactly what he had promised two thousand years earlier. We didn't have just one miracle, but one after another. It had turned out to be the most miraculous Christmas I ever experienced.

As I watched the last truck drive down the dusty road, inside my head I heard the words and I think Jesus spoke to me: "I told you not to worry."

44. A Christmas Miracle

Sheila Wipperman

WE DIDN'T WANT CHRISTMAS DAY TO BE LIKE THOSE WE had experienced during the past twenty years. While my sister and I were growing up, Christmas had been special. That was before our parents divorced. After that, Christmas lost its specialness for me.

After thirty years of marriage, my parents had divorced. Mom was so hurt that she warned us if we ever saw or talked to our dad, she wouldn't speak to us again. Dad secretly visited us for a few months, but knowing how things were, he eventually stopped.

Several years after their divorce, my sister and I married and started families of our own. Dad missed weddings and childbirths because Mom wouldn't have come if he had been present. Trying to talk to Mom about it was futile. Bitterness affects the entire family, but the one who suffers most is the person who harbors it. We saw firsthand that a bitter spirit poisons the heart and steals the joy from life. Not knowing what else to do, we prayed that the situation would change.

Nothing changed. Mom still wouldn't let us talk about Dad.

I suppose I stopped hoping. I know I stopped praying for her to change.

In 1989, my husband, Paul, and I decided to put our house up for sale. After an open house one weekend, our realtor told us that my dad, also a realtor, had come through not knowing it was our home. He noticed a sign on our fridge indicating that we were, in his words, "religious." A couple of weeks later, while we were out on a Sunday drive, I saw my dad placing an open-house sign on a property he was about to show.

"Look! That's my dad!" I yelled to Paul.

"What a coincidence," he said.

"This is no coincidence. We have to stop."

We honked, got his attention, and he waved at us. As soon as my husband stopped the car, I threw open the car door, grabbed my two children, and we rushed to see Dad.

He was elated to see us, and most of all, excited to meet his two grandchildren for the first time.

Afterward I called my sister and told her about the unexpected meeting. "Dad wants to know if you'll see him."

"I'll think about it." After we talked a few minutes, she said, "Yes! Yes!"

That was the beginning of our reconnection with Dad. Of course, we didn't tell Mom. That Christmas we wanted to invite Dad to join us, especially since he was alone. After all those years as a divided family, my brother-in-law, Jim, volunteered to talk with Mom. "Maybe I should be the one to try to talk some sense into her."

He went to see her. After using all the arguments of how

unfair it was that Dad couldn't see his kids or grandkids and why couldn't we be gracious enough to spend one day of the year together, he stopped talking and waited for her to answer.

"It's your house. Do what you like."

At least she hadn't said she wouldn't come if he did. That gave us hope.

On Christmas Day, we drove to my sister's home. We wondered and prayed about what would happen. Would it be fireworks or stony silence? "Dear God," I prayed, "let us have a true Christmas together."

When we got there, Mom had already arrived. She seemed to be in a festive mood. That was good. But how would she react when she saw Dad?

When Dad came into the house my sister and I, along with our spouses, were shocked as we watched our parents talk, joke, and laugh together. It was as if we weren't in the room with them. They caught up on events of the years they had been apart. It seemed natural and relaxed, as though nothing had happened in the twenty-year interim. My husband and I had prayed that Mom would at least be civil, but this was beyond anything we had prayed for or expected.

By the end of Christmas Day, we had yet another shock: Mom and Dad decided they wanted to see each other again. They meant dating. We could hardly believe it. I turned away from the others and silently thanked God for the amazing turn of events.

Four weeks later, came the best news. At the ages of seventy-four and eighty-one, our parents caught a ferry and traveled to the small town where they met fifty years earlier. *They eloped.*

When they announced their remarriage, we congratulated them. We also lovingly scolded them for not inviting us to the ceremony.

"We decided we were too old to make a fuss," Mom said.

"You're together," I said with tears in my eyes. "That's what's important."

That was the best Christmas ever. There was the miracle of our parents' reconciliation—something none of us had expected to happen. We had prayed for harmony and received an even greater blessing. God can change people so that they forgive those who have hurt them.

Something else happened that Christmas. I had prayed before—it was part of my life—but I hadn't had such a dramatic answer to prayer before. The dramatic answer to prayer was a miracle that increased my faith in a loving, caring God.

45. Miracles in a Box

Jane McBride Choate

IT HAD BEEN A ROUGH YEAR FOR OUR FAMILY, CULMINATING in the death of my mother after she had fought a lengthy battle with breast cancer. My husband's fledgling business barely paid him a salary. When I became discouraged, he reminded me that we were building for the future. But what of the present? I wanted to ask.

My writing brought in a small amount, but hardly enough to support our family of seven. Royalties arrived sporadically, and when they did, they were invariably smaller than I'd expected. My romance-writer's roots made it easy for me to joke that we were living on love mixed with a large dose of beans and rice.

An unexpected car repair took a large chunk out of our already depleted savings. My spirits plummeted in direct proportion to our plunging finances. I reminded myself that money didn't equal happiness, and lack of money didn't equal unhappiness. Those thoughts did little to improve my dim outlook.

I counted our blessings and tried to make a game out of it with our children. We had the big three, I reminded them and myself: faith, family, and friends. Still, I pictured a bleak holiday season. I couldn't summon the energy to do more than the minimum. What we needed was a Christmas miracle. However, I didn't see one in sight.

One raw morning, shortly before Christmas, my son rose early to deliver the papers on his route. He returned within a few seconds, carrying a large cardboard box. "Mom, look what I found by the front door."

Eagerly, he and the other children opened the box to reveal a turkey, loaves of homemade bread, a jar of honey, real butter, cans of pumpkin-pie filling, a sack of fresh vegetables, and all the other fixings for a holiday feast, right down to several small plastic bags containing spices.

My children yelled and whooped in celebration. Tears filled my eyes and I thanked God. "I wonder who gave this," I said. I thought of the love that went into preparing that gift. We checked the box for any way to identify the generous giver. We found none. Obviously the giver chose to remain anonymous, and we knew we should honor that desire and not try to discover the person's identity.

The children and I eagerly ate homemade bread, and that was a treat. We cut a loaf into thick slabs, slathered them with honey and butter, and savored each bite. We put the other items away for our Christmas feast.

The miracle box, as I chose to call it, reminded me about what truly mattered. I looked at neighbors, friends, and church members with a new attitude. Any one of them could have left the box on our porch. As a consequence, my warmth extended to almost everyone I encountered. I remembered to say thank you more often to family members, friends, and, most important, to our Creator, the ultimate author of all miracles.

Not unexpectedly, as I expressed my gratitude more frequently, I found more for which to be grateful. The miracle didn't occur with the arrival of the box of food on our doorstep, although it brightened our holidays and spirits immeasurably. The miracle occurred with the change inside my own heart.

I no longer concentrated on what was wrong in my life, but focused on what was right. I looked beyond myself to others. Could I work to make the holidays brighter for my husband who worked so hard to support us? For my children who did without new clothes and toys without complaint? Could I do something for the seventy-something-year-old widow in our church who would be alone for the Christmas season? What of my recently widowed father? The list continued as more names came to mind.

Despite limited resources and extremely limited sewing skills, I made a quilt for my daughter, found a few toys greatly marked down in an end-of-season sale for my sons, and contributed canned goods to a local food drive for needy families. My widowed friend had difficulty driving so I took her to the grocery store. It was a small gesture, but it provided a pleasant outing for both of us. My father was delighted with special letters from his daughter and grandchildren.

The new me acknowledged that I hadn't changed our circumstances; I had changed my attitude. I stopped thinking of our family as needy: I started seeing us as richly blessed.

My cheerfulness affected others, which spread throughout our family, touching my children and husband, friends, our mail carrier, the clerk at the checkout counter at the grocery store, the minister of our church. Our finances remained the same for another year, but I felt wealthy beyond measure.

I never learned the identity of our mysterious benefactor, but I saw him or her in every face, every pair of eyes, and every smile.

I had my Christmas miracle after all.

46. It Took a Miracle

Emila Belk

"THE DOCTOR THINKS YOUR DAD MIGHT HAVE LOU GEHRIG'S disease."

Our college-age son, Ryan, had been home for the Christmas holiday only minutes before we told him. "I thought you were going to give me good news," he said, "that Dad got a job or something happy like that."

A job for Steve would have been cause for celebration. Instead we added another big concern to our growing list.

Steve had experienced a series of difficult circumstances over the previous few years. After selling his vending company, a company he'd built for twenty years, he had trouble finding a good job that matched his skills. Unusual health problems caused him to be hospitalized and he went three and a half years without a full-time job.

Finally, Steve was hired for what seemed a perfect fit as manager for a delivery company. He felt relieved and happy to earn a steady income once again.

After four months on the job, Steve fell from a ladder and seriously injured his right arm. He needed an extensive surgical procedure that required plates and screws to piece his arm together. Because he was no longer able to meet the demands of his job, his employer terminated him.

Ten months later, one of the plates in his arm broke. That required another extensive surgery and a bone graft. After twenty-five months' healing time, including many of them in a cast, the use of a bone stimulator, and multiple doctor appointments, my husband returned to the doctor. That was his final appointment and he looked forward to being able to work without restrictions.

Steve didn't get his release.

As part of the test, the orthopedic surgeon handed the grip device to Steve. "Let's test your grip strength. Put this in your left hand and squeeze. We'll check your good arm first to compare."

The needle barely moved.

The doctor, clearly agitated with Steve, slapped the device into his own hand and demonstrated how to use it. "Squeeze the handles like this."

"I'm squeezing as hard as I can," Steve said.

"And that's your good arm!" The doctor put the device in Steve's right hand. "Let's see what this one says."

The needle on the gauge barely moved.

"I want you to see a hand specialist and a neurologist."

The December appointment with the neurologist left us feeling numb. That's when we learned of Steve's possible diagnosis of Lou Gehrig's disease. Instead of entering the Christmas season in a celebratory mood, we were somber and reflective. Not knowing what the future held, we treasured each moment with family and friends.

Our next step was to see a specialist. We waited for a phone call and further instructions. Weeks passed by without a call. Each day spent waiting was another day wondering. How would this all end? What would the specialists discover? What did tomorrow hold? How would we pay our bills?

During the time Steve was unable to work, we accumulated heavy debts. My limited income wasn't enough to pay even the immediate bills. We couldn't make house payments or buy things we felt we needed. That's when we turned to food stamps and Medicaid.

I did my best to keep the household running and take care of Jesse, our young son.

Even on the darkest days, both of us reminded ourselves that God loved us. If God loved us, he would provide and get us through this black period.

After a couple of visits to the Mayo Clinic we learned that Steve didn't have Lou Gehrig's disease. But the diagnosis of inclusion body myositis—a rare, untreatable, and progressive disease that attacks the muscles and causes bodies to cripple—meant that Steve would probably never be able to work again.

The news discouraged Steve. Even worse, we didn't think he qualified for disability benefits. Still, we applied for them anyway.

And we waited.

We didn't know the outcome, but we prayed daily. While we

waited, amazing things happened. People stuffed cash into my purse or put it in my hand. We received anonymous gifts through the mail. Someone taped money to our van. I opened my laptop computer one afternoon and found cash inside.

We received gift certificates for gas, groceries, and clothes. Our son's private school held a fund-raiser that covered his tuition. My hairdresser cut and styled my hair for free. One day the butcher at a local grocery store called. "I have a box of meat waiting for you." A friend plowed our driveway whenever it snowed. Even without applying, I received a job offer I felt I was born to do. And I could work from home.

Steve's spirits improved and both of us believed that God would provide for our needs.

A couple of days before Christmas, we received a notice in the mail. The government awarded Steve full disability benefits.

Getting disability benefits at Christmas felt like a miracle, but it wasn't the only miracle. In the months we had waited for the special Christmas gift, many people opened their hands and hearts to us.

In that one year, we had hit the emotional highs and lows. Yet even in the midst of the worst circumstances, Steve and I learned to trust God to provide for our needs.

47. Facing Failure at Christmas

Cecil Murphey

MY FATHER FAILED ME IN MANY WAYS. HE WAS AN ALCO-
holic. He regularly beat me. Even worse was that I didn't believe my father loved me. He never used the word *love*—I'm not
sure it was part of his vocabulary.

I left home at eighteen and I was in my early forties before I
faced the pain that had built up since childhood. During those
years I excused him by saying, "He did the best he could."

Perhaps that was true, but it resolved nothing. About six
months before he died, I had a strong feeling that if I didn't visit
him, I wouldn't see him alive again. Within a week I flew the
thousand miles to my hometown. It was difficult to find him
sober and alone, but on the second afternoon the house was
empty except for him and me.

I pulled my chair up next to his rocker. For perhaps twenty
minutes, I talked to him. "The one thing I've wanted from you
is to feel you loved me. If I knew that I could get past other
things." I didn't talk about the beatings or the verbal abuse. I
didn't expect my dad to change. I did hope, however, that he
would at least say he loved me or appreciated me—that he would
give me a kind or encouraging word.

When I paused, Dad got out of his rocking chair and walked out of the room. Behind me, the bedroom door closed. I sat in the empty room. Old, familiar feelings of rejection and anguish surged through me.

After that, he avoided me and we weren't alone again. He arranged for my nephew Larry to take me to the airport.

The following March, my mother called. "Your dad has had a stroke. He's in the hospital." When I asked if I should come, she suggested I wait. "We'll keep you informed." A few days later Dad was out of the hospital and home for a week. He suffered a second stroke. "This one seems worse," my mother said.

"I'll book the next flight." On the plane, I sensed I was already too late to see him alive. When I arrived at the airport, my nephew waited for me.

When I saw his face I knew. "Dad's dead, isn't he?"

Larry nodded. "About an hour ago."

I shed tears as I realized there would never be another opportunity for us to connect.

I went through the funeral with the family. One of his drinking buddies said, "Your dad was proud of you. He talked a lot about you." He told me some of the things Dad told them.

"I wish he'd said some of those things to me," I said when I stopped crying.

Afterward, I kept thinking of the many ways Dad had failed me. Apparently, he hadn't hated me, but how could I have known? He had been proud of me and what I had accomplished in my life, but he had never given me the slightest sign.

For seven or eight months I struggled with my pain. I wanted to forgive him, but it was difficult. Too many painful memories blocked me. I had tried when I visited him and he thwarted me. It took me several months to be able to say, "Dad, I forgive you." And when I said those words I meant it.

The year my father died, we celebrated Christmas Eve with our children. As we sat in a circle, I stared at the tree and the decorations, feeling grateful to the season. I silently thanked God for my family. Together we sang "O Come, All Ye Faithful."

As my gaze moved around the circle, I thought about Dad failing me and that I also had failed my children. I hadn't always been physically available; I was busy making a living and staying on the go. There were times when I could have hugged my three kids more, listened more attentively, or just hung out with them.

I had resolved the issues with Dad, but what about the issues with my children? After I died, would they have to struggle over forgiving me? I wanted them to be able to forgive me while I was still alive.

Before we opened presents, I told them of my battle to forgive my dad, but that I had finally succeeded. "I've failed you in many ways, and I don't want you to have to go through what I did. Please forgive me. I don't want you to struggle with forgiving me after I'm dead. Please tell me now where I've hurt or failed you and forgive me."

When I finished, I closed my eyes and waited for their outbursts of pain. I silently prayed that they would be able to forgive me.

Wanda, our oldest, had always been the sensitive one. "You aren't perfect," she said, "but you've always tried to be a good father."

John Mark, our youngest, shrugged. He was the quiet one and it meant he was all right.

When I spoke, I had particularly thought of Cecile, our middle child. She had been the rebel of the family and seemed to be in and out of trouble until she met Alan, the man she married. I worried more about her than the others. I felt that of all the kids, I had failed her the most.

After a long silence, Cecile said, "I remember that no matter what I did, you always loved me." Tears streamed down her cheeks.

Then my tears flowed.

I learned a valuable lesson that Christmas Eve. I had focused on my failures and the things I did wrong; my children focused on my love for them and what I did right. My children knew I loved them and that knowledge enabled them to forgive my shortcomings.

What was the miracle for me that Christmas Eve? I didn't have to be a perfect parent; I only had to be a loving father. I did my best parenting by the way I lived and they didn't judge me by the mistakes I'd made.

That was a night of miracles, but like many significant things in life, we don't grasp their impact until much later.

48. Sean's Question

Sara Zinn

I WASN'T PREPARED FOR OUR SON'S QUESTION. HE WAS ONLY four years old so it didn't seem that significant. I thought it was cute and laughed it off. Part of the surprise was that we weren't church people and our two sons had had a limited amount of Christian influence. I have no idea what prompted that question.

"When I go to heaven, will you and Daddy come and visit me there?" Sean stared at me and waited for an answer.

When I didn't respond, he asked, "Will you?"

"Yes, dear, you don't need to worry. We'll visit you."

My words satisfied him so he went out to play. At the time I didn't think much about what he asked.

Sean had been born with a heart murmur and doctors told us that many children outgrow the defect. He did everything any other boy of his age did, and he hadn't shown any special religious interest. I would probably have forgotten his insistent question except for what happened just before Christmas.

At a family Christmas party, my husband, Jerry, and I had a delightful time with Sean and his two-year-old brother, Chad. The room was filled with food and laughter. After dinner we had square dancing and nearly everyone tried it, including the children. Relatives snapped pictures. Everyone appeared to be having a wonderful time.

"What's wrong with Sean?" a girl called out.

"Is Sean dead?" a boy asked.

I ran over to where our son lay on the floor. Jerry and I and others tried to rouse him, but Sean didn't respond. Someone called 911. My uncle and others administered CPR. They weren't able to get any response.

This can't be happening to Sean. He's our son and we love him. I hadn't prayed since I was a child, but I silently cried out, *God, if you can hear me, please help our son.*

In what seemed like an extremely long time, but probably was only minutes, a team of paramedics arrived. They worked on Sean and seemed determined not to give up. One of them used a defibrillator to shock his heart.

One of the paramedics asked about his health history, his doctor, and medication. They rushed him to the nearest hospital. We prepared to follow the ambulance. Just before we left, I rushed over to an uncle, who I knew was a serious Christian, and begged him, "Please pray for Sean."

"I've already been praying," he said. "I'll continue to pray."

At the hospital, a young doctor ran into the room where they had taken our son. Minutes later, the doctor came out to see us. "We're going to try to put in a pacemaker," he said and hurried away. Not long afterward, the same doctor came back out, looked at Jerry and me, and said, "I'm sorry. We weren't able to save your little boy."

"No, no," I said repeatedly. The tears flowed and I couldn't stop them.

A nurse led us to a chapel where we could begin the grieving process. It felt as though the loss of Sean had sucked the life from my soul. The nurse gave me a tranquilizer and I was able to calm down.

We left the hospital, but Jerry and I didn't sleep much Christmas Eve. The next day the grief hit us. I couldn't stop crying. We sat with family members, crying, talking, questioning, and searching for answers.

Many relatives and friends tried to comfort us, but the one person I most remember was a friend of my aunt named Mary Lou. She came to our house and spent Christmas Day with us. Several times she put her arms around each of us and listened when we talked and held us when we cried. She also prayed with us. She spoke of Jesus as though he was her best friend and was in the room with us.

She let me know that it was all right for me to pray, so I did. I prayed from the depths of my heart. I can't explain in words, but a change came over me. I believed in a loving God and was at peace.

Later on Christmas Day, Mary Lou's husband came to our house. He was kind and gentle and expressed his love. A number of people, many whom I hadn't known, reached out to us. Because of the change that had come over me, I began to think of them as the physical arms of Jesus that enfolded us.

The people in a small church in our town that Jerry and I had avoided for years reached out to us. Through a small-group study and their personal visits, they became a life-line to us.

Because of their human love, I became convinced of a divine love that understood how I felt. Many times I thought, God watched while his own son died. Surely he could feel the pain inside my heart. Because of the death of his son on earth, my son would live in heaven.

Thirty years later, the miracle of the Christmas season still holds a double meaning for me. That was the time when we lost our son; that was the time we found God's loving son in our lives.

I can still hear Sean's question, "When I go to heaven, will you and Daddy come and visit me there?"

I can answer with complete certainty, "Yes, my precious son, I'll visit you and stay with you in heaven."

Who We Are

Cecil Murphey has written or cowritten more than one hundred books, including *The New York Times* best seller, *90 Minutes in Heaven*. He writes on a variety of subjects including caregiving, aging, spiritual growth, and male sexual abuse. Contact him at www.cecilmurphey.com or www.themanbe hindthewords.com.

Marley Gibson is a young-adult author whose first published books in the *Sorority 101* series were released by Puffin Speak Books (Penguin Group) under the pen name Kate Harmon. The books are *Sorority 101: Zeta Or Omega?* and *Sorority 101: The New Sisters*. Her new *Ghost Huntress* series, written under her own name, from Houghton Mifflin Harcourt's Graphia Line, are *The Awakening*, *The Guidance*, and *The Reason*. She can be found online at www.marleygibson.com, her blog at www.books boysbuzz.com, or at www.myspace.com/mhgibson.

Denise Aulie is a devoted wife and mother of five. She has served as a missionary to indigenous peoples in Mexico for thirty years. Her life's call is to encourage others through relationships, writing, public speaking, and photography. You may e-mail her at deniseaulie7@gmail.com.

Twila Belk also known as the Gotta Tell Somebody Gal, is a speaker, writer, publicist, and conference director. She works closely with bestselling author Cecil Murphey as his manager and personal assistant. To learn more about Twila, visit www .gottatellsomebody.com.

Florence E. Blake has seen more than 650 of her nonfiction articles published in newspapers, magazines, and anthologies, including Guideposts books, *Mature Living*, and the *Boston Globe*. She also has composed seventeen songs, and teaches writing courses at Rogue Community College in Medford, Oregon.

Pam Bostwick's many articles appear in newspapers, magazines, and anthologies including *Chicken Soup for the Soul*. She enjoys her country home, loves the beach, plays guitar, and is a volunteer counselor. She has seven children and ten grandchildren and happily remarried on July 7, 2007. Please e-mail her at pamloves7@verizon.net.

Ingrid Briles works for the Salvation Army of Charleston, West Virginia, as their social service intake worker. Her publishing credits include the *Charleston Gazette*, *Magazine of Appalachian Women*, *Pond Ripples Christian E-zine*, and *Rat-*

tlesnake Review. She is a member of West Virginia Writers, Inc. She lives and writes in Charleston.

Renie Burghardt, who was born in Hungary, is a freelance writer with many writing credits. She has been published in several *Chicken Soup for the Soul* books, twenty-five Guideposts books, and other anthologies. She has also written for magazines such as *Angels on Earth, Mature Living, Cat Fancy, Pure Inspiration,* and *Missouri Life*. She lives in the country and loves nature, hiking, and spending time with family and friends. Visit her online at www.renieburghardtsworld.blogspot.com.

Jennifer Lynn Cary is the author of numerous pieces. Her work has been included in several anthologies including *God Answers Moms' Prayers, Life Savors for Women,* and *The One Year Life Verse Devotional*. She and her husband reside in Arizona.

Sandy Cathcart is a freelance writer, photographer, and artist living in the forests of southern Oregon. She enjoys the beauty of creation and connecting with the people of this great land. You can see a sample of her work at www.sandycathcart.com.

Jane McBride Choate has been weaving stories in her head ever since she can remember to entertain family and friends with tales of derring-do and knights in shining armor. Twenty-eight books and two hundred articles and short stories later, she still entertains others with her imagination.

Donna Dawson is a creative writing instructor at a local college in Ontario, Canada, and an award-winning writer. She writes romance, mystery, suspense, and thriller novels. You can find information about her books, *Fires of Fury* (Awe-struck Books), *Redeemed, The Adam & Eve Project* and *Vengeance* (Word Alive Press) at www.authordonnadawson.com.

Scoti Springfield Domeij has written more than two hundred articles on being single, parenting, divorce, faith, and caregiving. She is the author of five books and coauthored *Wrong Way, Jonah!* Scoti helps single parents throw off fear, embrace new life, and courageously lead their families to draw on their God-given abilities. Visit her at www.scotidomeij.com or www.courageoussingleparenting.blogspot.com.

Shawnelle Eliasen has been writing since 2008. She's been published in *Hearts at Home* magazine and *Guideposts*. She writes about life, family, friendship, and God's grace. You can reach her at seliasen@frontiernet.net.

Dianna Graveman holds an MFA degree in writing and a bachelor's degree in education. She is an editor, award-winning writer, and a teacher. Her writing recognition includes awards from Missouri Writers Guild and Catholic Press Association. You can contact her through www.diannagraveman.com and www.gravemanbooks.com.

Sunny Marie Hackman enchants, motivates, and transports her audiences by chronicling the "funprints" of God in the lives of the obscure and famous. Since 1999, she has shared her stories with others across the country as an author, speaker, and living history presenter of Minnie Pearl. Contact her at sunnymariehackman@earthlink.net.

Jean Matthew Hall is a freelance writer. Her stories and articles appear in a variety of magazines and anthologies including *The Embrace of a Father, Whispering in God's Ear, Chicken Soup for the Chocolate Lover's Soul,* and *The Ultimate Gardener.* She blogs My Conversations with God at www.jeanmat thewhall.blogspot.com.

Elizabeth M. Harbuck is a mother, teacher, wife, grandmother, and an accomplished musician. Her love of music and the Bible have been coupled together for more than fifty years of her life, serving many churches as organist and choir director. She is widely recognized throughout the South for her violin and piano talents, as well as her patient teaching skills to children.

Drienie Hattingh was born and raised in South Africa. She immigrated to America in 1986. Her columns and stories have been published in newspapers and magazines in Minnesota, Utah, California, and South Africa. Drienie lives in Eden, Utah, with her husband, their spoiled little dog, and a seasonal moose in the Wasatch Mountains.

Fred W. Iverson is seventy-one and recovering from a brainstem stroke. He feels he is alive only because of God's blessing.

Iverson has previously self-published a booklet of teenage questions about God.

Laurie Kolp is an award-winning freelance writer, mother of three, and graduate of Texas A&M University. She honed her writing skills during her twelve-year career as a language arts teacher. She is a member of the Golden Triangle Writer's Guild and writes short stories, children's books, poetry, novels, and her blog. You can reach her at www.conversationswithacardinal.blogspot.com or via e-mail at lkkolpbmt@yahoo.com.

Madeleine Kuderick balances parenting, career, and her love of writing on Florida's Gulf Coast where she lives with her husband, two children, and a menagerie of pets. She hopes to inspire others who face the challenge of dyslexia. Learn more about her at www.madeleinekuderick.com.

Marcia Lee Laycock's inspirational writing has won awards in Canada and the United States. Her novel, *One Smooth Stone*, won the Best New Canadian Christian Author award in 2006. Marcia speaks at many women's events. Visit her at www.vinemarc.com.

Pamela J. McCann is an aspiring author of children's books and has several stories near completion. After many years of caring for various family members, she has returned to writing.

Beverly Hill McKinney is the author of more than seventy inspirational articles, including four anthologies. She's a regular contributor to the *Christian Journal* and is the published writer of church skits and curriculum and two self-published books. A graduate of the Jerry B. Jenkins Christian Writer's Guild, you can contact her at bmckinnehill@yahoo .com.

Shari McMinn and her husband slowed down their two-career lifestyle and moved to a remote farm. During the past seven years they have adopted five children. In addition to writing nonfiction, Shari is a master gardener, 4-H volunteer, and homeschools their eight youngest children.

Mary Kay Moody is a freelance writer with short stories in *All My Bad Habits I Learned from Grandpa, Long Ridge Writers Group 2004 Christmas Anthology,* articles in *Discipleship Journal,* and *Crest Sun.* She is currently writing a suspense series, and leads a domestic violence ministry at her church. Find her online at www.marykaymoody.com.

Violet Moore is the author of *In The Right Place* and *Moments of Meditation* and cocreator of Carr Twins & Co. (www .carrtwins.com) publishing. She is an inspirational writer and speaker and a featured contributor to an international women's ministry Web site. She is vice president of the California Writer's Club, Tri-Valley Branch.

Emily Osburne is the author of *Everyday Experts on Marriage* and writes primarily for young married couples. She and her husband, Clay, lead marriage workshops in the Greater Atlanta area.

Edwina Perkins is a homeschool mom of four and has served beside her minister-husband, David, for twenty-four years. A member of Word Weavers in Orlando, she is passionate about writing and speaking messages of hope to women. You can reach her via e-mail at Perkster6@earthlink.net or at theper kinspen.blogspot.com.

Kelly Carper Palden is a communications professional with twenty years experience as a contributor to a variety of businesses and nonprofit organizations (www.kellycarpercom munications.com). She is a freelance writer for numerous publications, and a first-time children's author of *Puppy Tales: The Adventures of Adam the Australian Shepherd*.

Phyllis Ring's articles and essays have appeared in such magazines as *American Profile, New Hampshire Home*, and *Writer's Digest*. A collection of her essays, *Life at First Sight: Finding the Divine in the Details* was a 2009 release. You can find her online at www.phyllisring.com.

Tracy Ruckman is a freelance writer, editor, and photographer. She owns Write Integrity Editorial Services and the popular Pix-N-Pens blog for writers and photographers. Visit her on the Web at: www.WriteIntegrity.com, www.pixnpens.com, or www.tracyruckman.com.

Jane Rumph is the author of *Stories from the Front Lines: Power Evangelism in Today's World* and *Signs and Wonders in America Today*. A freelance writer and editor, she has contributed to numerous books and periodicals, including *Charisma*, *Momentum*, and *The Upper Room*. She lives in Pasadena, California. You may contact her at www.janerumph.com.

Dave Schrader is the host of the popular paranormal talk radio show, *Darkness on the Edge of Town*. Each week, he explores the world of the paranormal and aims to educate, enlighten, and entertain people by speaking to experts in all fields of the paranormal. Dave is the father of six children and lives in Minnesota, where he hosts his show every Saturday and Sunday night on www.DarknessRadio.com.

Claudia Sadara of Tarpon Springs, Florida, has had articles, essays, short stories, poems, and songs published. She is currently working on composing her fourth piano instrumental CD of soothing, eclectic music. You can visit her online at www.geocities.com/Claudia_Sodaro.

Virginia B. Tenery has written numerous short stories, including "Adino," in the *Light at the Edge of Darkness* anthology. She also writes suspense novels. Contact her at vbhtenery@aol.com or vbhtenery@gmail.com.

Donna Teti has been published in *Guideposts* magazine and was a 2008 recipient of Guideposts Writer's Workshop Contest. She has created a Web site of her inspirational writings to encourage the grieving heart. Donna is married with three children and resides in West Chester, Pennsylvania. You may reach Donna at donnateti@verizon.net.

Cindy Thomson, author of *Brigid of Ireland, Celtic Wisdom: Treasures From Ireland*, and coauthor of *Three Fingers: The Mordecai Brown Story*, is a full-time freelance writer with an interest in history, family, and baseball. Visit her on the Web at www.cindyswriting.com.

Geni J. White reviews books for Thomas Nelson, Inc. and Asia-east. A freelance editor, she writes humor articles as Yenna Buchay and you can reach her at geniwhite.typepad.com/a_candle_in_the_dark.

Suzan L. Wiener has had numerous stories, articles, poems, and other shorter pieces accepted by magazines such as *Mature Living, Mature Years, Versus*, and *Reader's Digest*. She has written a love poetry e-book available at www.ereadable.com/scripts/browse.asp?ref=1602760330.

Kathy Winchell is a writer, drama teacher, and musical theater director. She is a contributor to *The Embrace of a Father*, and has completed two novels. She lives with her husband and two sons in Atlanta, Georgia. Contact her at Kwinchell4@gmail.com.

Sheila Wipperman has written anecdotes, articles, essays, and greeting cards. Other writing credits include *Reader's Digest*, Warner Press, Andrew McMeel Publishing, and Oatmeal Studios. She has won a number of writing contests, recently placing third in Gene Perret's "One Great Line" contest. E-mail her at whisper@telus.net.

Lisa-Anne Wooldridge is an author, speaker, and teacher who makes her home in the San Francisco Bay area with her husband, Andres, and their three miracles, Jesse, Ivy, and Blaze. Visit her at www.Lisa-Anne.net.

Sara Zinn is a speaker, writer, and a mentor with the Big Brothers/Big Sisters program. She is a licensed clinical counselor with a private practice in Athens, Ohio, specializing in marriage and family counseling. Sara is a wife, mother, and grandmother. She and her husband, Jerry, have been married thirty-seven years.